The Anti-Procrastination Mentality

How to Stop Being Lazy and Get Things Done

Dan Kristoph

Published by Krister Publishing

TABLE OF CONTENTS

Your Free Gift... 7

Foreword: Why Is It So Hard to Be Motivated to Work? 9

The History of Procrastination: The Caveman Brain.... 11

The Laziness Enjoyment 13

No Gain, No Pain? 15

The Book Structure 17

PART 1: THE RELATIONSHIP

The So No Good Relationship Between Procrastination and Our Success.....................21

Slowdown of Progress 23

Failure Flirt 25

Catalyst of Quitting 27

PART 2: THE DEFINITION

The 3Cs that Define Our Anti-Procrastination Mentality 31

The Cause.. 32

The Consistency 35

The Continuation 37

PART 3: THE APPROACHES (MOTIVATION-BUILD-FOCUS)

Three Anti-Procrastination Mentality Pillars: Motivation, Habit, Focus 41

Motivation Build 1 – Cause: Get the Powerful Targets 47

Question the Push.. 48

Make Targets Prioritization................................ 51

Think About Everyone 54

Motivation Build 2 – Consistency: Optimize Your Work Context 57

Adjust the Workplace 58

Understand Your Optimal Time 61

Practice the Preferable Method...................... 63

Motivation Build 3 – Continuation: Compare Current Condition.. 67

Compare with Your Ideal Self........................ 69

Compare with Your Peers 71

Compare with Successful People 73

Habit Build 1 – Cause: Track Progress and Reflect 77

Set Big Day Appraisal.. 78

Refine the Approach 81

Take Time to Evaluate Daily 83

Habit Build 2 – Consistency: Formulate Work Schedule **87**

Divide the Work and Relaxation Hours......................... 89

Determine Weekly and Daily Details 91

Implement with Discipline 94

Habit Build 3 – Continuation: Shape the Bullet Proof Mentality...**97**

Fail Early, Succeed Early.. 99

Formulate and Implement the Way Out Soon 101

Place the Time to Get Back.. 103

Focus Build 1 – Cause: Sharpen Your Goals **107**

Think Big, Pick Small.. 108

Set Up Gradual Targets 110

Consider the Time.. 113

Focus Build 2 – Consistency: Move Away from Distractions **117**

Define the Things That Disturb You 119

Clear Your Thoughts 121

Set Up the Barrier 123

Focus Build 3 – Continuation: Look at the Positive **127**

See the Progress and Keep Going 129

Learn and Move On.. 131

Get on With the Effort... 133

Final Words: When Will You Start Building the Mentality? 137

Did You Like the Anti-Procrastination Mentality? 141

More Books by Dan Kristoph 143

About the Author 145

YOUR FREE GIFT

As a way to say thank you for choosing to read one of my books, I offer you to download my free e-book with the title of "**23 Good Habits in Life: The Simple Routine Practices that Can Make You More Positive, Happy, and Successful**". It is an 80-pages comprehensive e-book that will tell you about why good habits can be important to make you a more positive, happy, and successful person, what is the definition of good and bad habits, and also the 23 good simple habits which I think are among the most positively impactful in life that you should implement consistently. This free but valuable e-book might be the thing that you need to start implementing more good habits and less bad habits in life.

To grab your copy, you can visit the link below and join my email list:
https://positivitystories.com/free-gift

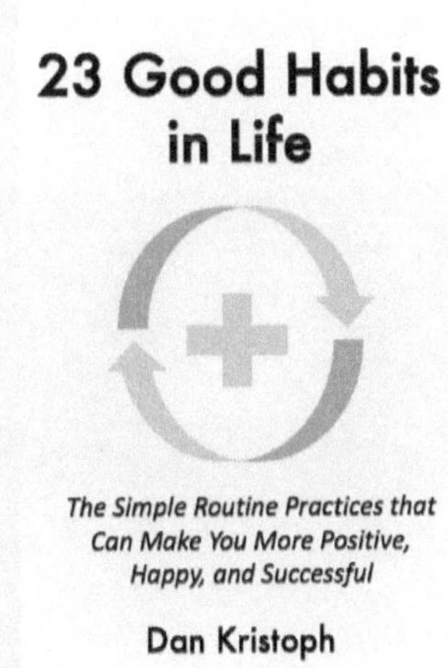

In the following pages, you will learn about the danger that you should know about procrastination that can prevent us to succeed in life, what are the 3Cs that can define an anti-procrastination mentality which will make you far more resistant to the urge of procrastination, and how to build the pillars that will support those 3Cs for a strong anti-procrastination mentality.

So, without further ado, let's dive in.

FOREWORD: WHY IS IT SO HARD TO BE MOTIVATED TO WORK?

Enjoying the time by relaxing and not doing anything related to work is something great, right?

Let's imagine that you are in your house. Just sleeping and resting yourself until you get bored of it. Then, when you are done with your resting, you can do anything that you want to do to spend your time with. You can play the games that you desire all day, go out with your friends to some places where you can have a great time together, or, if movies are the things that you like, watch some good movies that you have not watched yet (or you have. Well, it is sometimes fun to watch again some memorable ones). Whatever it is that you want to do, just do it. There is no one to stop you.

Then, after you are tired doing the activities that you like, you can just go to your bed again and rest until your energy is refreshed before you do the things that you want to again. This is the condition that you are going to experience every day. You just need to relax and don't do any work at all.

Sounds fun? You can bet on that. Most people want that kind of situation in their life where there is no need whatsoever to work every day.

Just need to relax and do the things that you desire.

Well, that wish that most of us have is one of the things that makes it so hard for us to find the motivation in ourselves to spend time every day with the work that we need to do daily.

You see, relaxation is something that we crave and love to do while work is something usually related to stress and an activity that we don't enjoy. Procrastination is the feeling that we get because of this preference.

We feel that it is better if we don't do the things that we don't want to do right now. We want to delay them as long as possible or even stop doing it if we have the possibility to.

After all, who wants to work when they don't have to, right?

Well, if only things can work out like that, then all of us can give in to the urge of procrastination and relax all the time without giving a care. Unfortunately, it does not work like that for most of us. You always have to work first to get something that you want before you can relax without having to worry about things like money to buy food with or the impact that we want to bring from the work that we do.

Work is something essential for all of us to do to gain the things that we desire. Hence, it is also essential that we need to have a strong anti-procrastination mentality if we want to do it properly. We need to push aside our desire to enjoy time with relaxing and doing other things that are far more enjoyable for us to work hard so we can get the results that we want from its process.

But it is very understandable, of course, if we often prefer to relax and enjoy our time rather than do the hard work that we need to do. We always feel happier by spending time relaxing rather than laboring, after all.

In fact, it is something that has been done for a long time ago by our ancestors. It is the time in history when most humans still lived in caves and they need to hunt almost every day as a process to get the food they need to eat.

The History of Procrastination: The Caveman Brain

When hunting is still the most dominant jobs in the world, the humans often need to roam to places to do it. The reason is because at times, the animals that they want to hunt and eat is scarcely available in the area near to them. So, they have to move and find the right spots where they can do the hunting process properly and get something to consume.

When they do that, though, it also can bring more danger to them as they look up for the animals that they want to kill. Humans are not on the very top level of the food chains, after all. Some animals hunt humans as well and so, the cavemen in that era need to be aware of the presence of those predators too in addition to finding the spots where there are animals that can be hunted.

When humans find their prey, it is not a straightforward process. It is not like they just go to the animal that they hunt and take it home. They have to chase it or do some other things so the animals can be killed and then taken to their cave. If they cannot hunt them properly, then there will be no food to eat for the day.

So, the humans roam in the wild, they have to be aware of the predators that also want to eat them during that time, they have to find their prey, and try to catch it before bring the food back home. That is a lot of time for humans to keep their awareness of. If at some time the predating animals come to the place where the humans are in the process to hunt some animals that they want to eat, then more often than not the humans will escape from the place and abandon the animals that they originally want to hunt. They don't complicate things, make the decision making simple, and see that the danger that they feel far outweigh the benefits that they can get by staying to do the hunting. The instinct in their brain rules the risk-averse strategy and they prefer to not risk being eaten than to have the chance to get the food that they want.

This kind of thinking is said by scientists to be one of the reasons why humans can keep the survival of their species until now. The risk-avoiding strategy makes it harder for us to be caught by the predators and it turns out that it is a good thing that explains why we are still alive in the world right now and dominates the world currently from other species.

The caveman brain that has this instinct, though, is being bequeathed to us, the humans of the modern world who don't need to go hunting anymore and get the risk of being eaten by some predators. As a result, we become risk-averse species mirroring our ancestors and that makes our brain dictates that something which can harm us as something that should be avoided at all cost.

This holds true when we want to do some work as the cavemen want to do some hunting in the past. When there is something that seems complicated and can bring a bad thing for us, whether it is the fear of failure, stress, or anything not good, then we prefer to avoid it and do other things that are simpler and more enjoyable to us. That is why we prefer to avoid doing hard work that can make us stress and have the possibility to bring us failure, rejection, doubt, and/or any other negative feeling.

Does that sound familiar? Well, you bet it is. That is what procrastination does to us. It turns out that procrastination has its history and that feeling comes from our cavemen ancestors who prefer to go for a simple and risk-free solution rather than the complicated and more dangerous one. They need it because they have to avoid predators so they will not get eaten and it is one of the keys for survival in that era. But for us to have this kind of instinct, it can be something contra productive and get us to the situation where we prefer to not think and work hard as the activity can potentially very rewarding to us but filled with the negative kinds of feeling like fear and doubt.

This kind of risk-averse instinct from the cavemen's brain proves useful for them but can be bad for us. Moreover, when we decide to give in to procrastination and enjoy our time by not working on something that we need to do, it can bring some happiness and enjoyment to us directly that no hard work can do to us, at least in short-term period.

The Laziness Enjoyment

As we imagine to relax and try to do the activities that we enjoy the most, what do we feel? One of the things that can be can come to our mind is the enjoyment feeling. After all, you wouldn't do what you do when you choose to procrastinate if it is something that is not going to bring you a happy feeling. It will be just the same as work if it does the opposite, right?

The laziness that is done by relaxing, delaying, and forgetting about the work that we need to do is so captivating for most people for a reason. Compared to the dizziness and boring feeling that we get when we do the difficult tasks that we need to do, it seems like an easy choice to just not trying. We decide fully on giving in to procrastination.

Thus, that kind of situation makes it needs a little to no push for us to just relax and do the things that we want to do. The enjoyment that we get from laziness is already some kind of reward that we get almost immediately after we choose to be idle. It is a stark contrast compared to the hard work activity when the reward is usually long-term and we don't know if or when we are going to achieve success after the work that we do. It can take a long time to achieve success and we, as humans, prefer to go for things that will yield immediate and clear return to us.

That is all logical and so, it is very enjoyable to do some laziness in most of the time that we have. Try to think about it. When you have to choose the thing that you can get the benefit immediately and that benefit is a certain thing versus something that you can get only get the outcome that you want after you do it for a long time constantly, the period that you need to do it to get the reward is uncertain, and there is always a risk that you will not get what you want even after doing it all the time, which one do you choose? Well, that is procrastination versus work and from that one-sided description, it is clear which one that we mostly choose. It is the choice that most people made, in fact, every day. When they don't have any obligation to work, they just not do it because it is not enjoyable. Laziness is a sure thing in comparison and it gives you something that you can feel right away.

Well, there is always a catch to it, though. It is short term versus long term thing and when you choose laziness, it can directly make you feel happy but in the long term, it will be no good for you in terms of the big things that you want to achieve in life and the financial needs that you want to fulfill. Work can offer those things and although it is often risky and stressful, it can lead you to the achievements that you want as long as you keep trying until you get it.

But, of course, it is still quite an abstract thing, right? You still don't know when you will get the rewards of your hard work and it can bring you stress while waiting. The immediate enjoyment coming from choosing procrastination can be the thing that you decide to have most of the time rather than having to do hard work that can be pretty tedious.

When it comes to the success that you can achieve through the hard work that you do, it comes with a lot of pain to put in the effort to do it and keep the work consistent. And we know that procrastination gives no pain and you can do it with no to little bad things attached to it, at least for the short term.

No Gain, No Pain?
Ever heard of that famous phrase, no pain no gain?

It is a catchy phrase that we quite often hear in the world of weight loss activities. You cannot lose weight if you don't do the work out activity consistently. The translation to other activities than weight loss is: you cannot gain the things that you want without some sacrifice and pain that you need to bear in order to get it.

Well, when you do some procrastination, the terms must be no gain no pain, then. In terms of doing procrastination, if we choose to not have the things that we want, then we will not feel the pain that is required to attain that, right? We can just relax all day and do the things that we want to do without having to worry about anything.

If your current situation is where that you want to be and you do not have any other ambition that can give you the motivation to push further to maintain and improve on the condition that you have currently, then you may want to choose to procrastinate and abandon the hard work that you need to do. After all, you are already in the state that you desire then there is no need to work again as there are no goals that you need to chase.

Well, that is the ideal situation. When you don't need to gain anything, then you don't have to go through the pain to gain it. Work hard constantly to achieve the things that you want takes a lot of sacrifices and choose to procrastinate instead will save you from that.

But most of the time it does not work that way for us, unfortunately. As a human, you always have the things that you want to achieve and that can only be done by the effort that you put in. You cannot just be lazy and hope that good things will find its way to you.

Even when you have already achieved the success that you want and you are already in the state that people want to be, often you need to maintain that and even want to improve further by gaining more success. After all, most of the time you don't get to that state without any consistent hard work and you will not feel comfortable if you need to abandon the habit that you already have in terms of working hard constantly.

Procrastination is something very enjoyable to do and relaxing or doing the things that we want to spend our time with can be pain-free and give us the enjoyment that we want right away. But it is not productive and good for you to have the mindset that prefers procrastination all the time. Hard work, on the other hand, is something that we need to do consistently if we want to achieve something meaningful in life and the habit of this can be great for us. Even if hard work is something that cannot be predicted exactly when it is going to bear the fruits that you want to have, keep on going with continuous effort and constant improvement should guarantee you to have success at some point in the future.

Therefore, to get the most from life and accomplish the things that we desire, we need a strong anti-procrastination mentality inside of us. We need to do our hard work before we can think about relaxing and doing nothing.

The Book Structure
Because of that, this book called The Anti-Procrastination Mentality – How to Stop Being Lazy and Get Things done is written to help you build that kind of mentality to utilize the most of your time and have the work that you need to do completed.

To answer to that purpose and to let you have a complete understanding on anti-procrastination mentality, this book is organized and structured with the description as follows:

The So No Good Relationship Between Procrastination and Our Success – This first part will discuss how procrastination can be the thing that most detrimental to us in terms of achieving the success that we want. This part is written so you have it in your mindset on why you really need to adopt anti-procrastination mentality.

The 3Cs That Defines Anti-Procrastination Mentality – Three things can help you in defining the strong anti-procrastination mentality that we want. We call it the 3Cs: Cause, Consistency, and Continuation. We will discuss each of them in detail on how they contribute to the anti-procrastination mentality in this part.

Three Anti-Procrastination Mentality Pillars: Motivation, Habit, Focus – These three pillars can be big in helping you to shape the 3Cs that defines the Anti-Procrastination Mentality. We will take a look more at how each of them can support you in building a strong anti-procrastination mentality in this chapter.

Motivation Build 1 – Cause: Get the Powerful Targets – Each part of the pillar must be built well to help you to get things done optimally. We divide each pillar in the book and see the way how can they be built to shape each of the three Cs for you in detail. The first part of the division is the motivation build for your cause: how to define powerful targets that can make you stay driven to do hard work.

Motivation Build 2 – Consistency: Optimize Work Context – What is the way you can build the motivation to stay consistent with your work? Getting your work context to fuel the consistency can help you tremendously with it. This chapter will discuss deeper about how that can be done to your work context.

Motivation Build 3 – Continuation: Compare Current Condition – Comparison can be good or bad for us depending to the way we utilize the result. In this chapter, we will see how it can be done in a good way to support the continuation in your work despite the struggles that you need to face.

Habit Build 1 – Cause: Track Progress and Reflect – Knowing where you are currently in terms of your work periodically can help you to have the motivation to stay working so you can gain more progress. We will see how that kind of result and progress tracking can be done to support your anti-procrastination mentality.

Habit Build 2 - Consistency: Formulate Work Schedule – Having some kind of formula to be the guidance of when to work and when to relax can be one of the most important things to hold the urge to procrastinate in the time when you should work. We will talk about how you can formulate a work schedule that can help you work consistently when it is time to work.

Habit Build 3 – Continuation: Shape the Bullet Proof Mentality – The habit to get back up again as soon as possible when there are problems in your work and solve them completely should be something that can prevent you to procrastinate when things get tough in your labor. We will discuss how you can shape a habit that helps you to do something like that.

Focus Build 1 – Cause: Sharpen Your Goals - Being selective in the goals that you want to chase can be the formulation of a strong motivation to work as you don't need to get the headache of having too many things to focus on. This chapter will see what is the recommended process to select your goals so they can help you to achieve them.

Focus Build 2 – Consistency: Move Away from Distractions – You are always prone to procrastinate when you can access the things that distract you from your work. In this part, we will see how you can minimize those distractions for your work.

Focus Build 3 – Continuation: Look at the Positive – Maintaining a positive mindset on the struggles that you meet in work can help you to keep on going and abandon the urge to quit your work. This part will try to help you understand how you can build the mindset to always try to look on the positive and not procrastinate because of the negatives from the bad experience that you need to go through in work.

By going through all the contents above in the book, I hope that you can build a strong anti-procrastination mentality that always tries its best to get the job done and can optimize the time that you have, whether it is to work when you need to work or it is to rest when you need to relax.

Let's get to it by starting the first part.

THE SO NO GOOD RELATIONSHIP BETWEEN PROCRASTINATION AND OUR SUCCESS

There is a bad relationship between our laziness and our achievements. That friction has been going for years and it seems that the relationship will never be amended unfortunately.

When you want to achieve success in life, whatever your definition of that success is, you will be very excited about the possibility that you can have when you eventually realize the success. For example, if your definition of success is to be the richest person in the world, then you will think of the possibility that you can have by achieving that dream. You can buy things that you want, travel to wherever place that you desire, or have any house or car that you like.

Everything seems good for you. Now, you just need to find a way to realize that dream of yours.

And that is when the hard part comes in.

If you want to get the success, then you have to work constantly to do that. But often when we see how much workload that we need to do to achieve the success or when we finally have a clear idea about what should be done to attain the achievement, we feel lazy and do not have enough motivation to start doing the things that are needed to be worked on. Even if we have the initial motivation and start to work on that, we can feel bored in the middle of the constant work that we need to do or feel that it is not worth our time when we face some struggles or problems in the road to success. The work that we need to do can be seen as too complicated too much for us and that makes us not having the urge again to do the constant hard work to achieve the success that we desire.

That is what procrastination is and it can have a very negative effect on the chance of us realizing our success in our work.

When we have a high urge for procrastination and we give in to that, then we will delay or abandon the work that needs to be done and just relax or do other fun things with the time that we have. When you see the fact that success needs some high degree of effort, often in a long time, to make it comes to you, then you know that just relax or having fun without doing any work at all cannot be good for your chance to achieve it.

Therefore, procrastination can be one of the main things that keeps you far away from the success that you want to have. It is because having that can make you feel that you don't have enough motivation to work hard to get the achievements that you want to have.

Such as the relationship between procrastination and our success. When we have many amounts of one side, then we need to reduce much from the other side because they are not compatible with each other. If you give in to procrastination too much, then you can say goodbye to the big things that you want to accomplish in life. If you don't stop working despite the urge to procrastinate that you may have during your work, then you are sure to have a much greater chance of success.

That nature of the relationship between procrastination and success is shaped from three things that are caused by procrastination: the slowdown for the progress in our road to success, the increased likelihood of failure because of it, and the likely catalyst for our decision to quit in trying to chase for the things that we want to achieve in life. We will discuss more about why they are important contributors in the breakdown of the relationship in the following parts of the chapter.

Slowdown of Progress

Success is attained by the cumulative efforts that are being done by a person or people consistently over time. There is no such thing as an "overnight success". When you see a story like that from a successful person, then there is a high amount of constant effort behind it that takes him/her years to accumulate before he/she can get to the position where he/she is now.

Therefore, if we keep on putting in the effort every day to realize our goals, then they should come closer and closer to us as a result. Now, what happens when there is a huge urge to procrastinate when we do our work, we choose to give in to it and abandon the things that we currently work on?

As you may have guessed, that decision will hinder our advancement to get the things that we want. The way that is being done is by delaying or even stopping us from doing the hard work to spend our time with and instead, we will just relax or do other things that are completely unrelated to our work.

Now, the relaxing activities can be good and you should spend some of the time that you have to do it in order to recharge yourself after all the hard work that you have done. However, you should not do it most of the time, especially in the time when you need to work. Instead, you should spend your time to try to be consistent on putting in the effort that you need to get you closer to the success that you want.

Success requires works and time, that is for sure. Lots of them. When you give in to procrastination and not spending your working hours doing the hard work that you need to, then you will make your progress slower or even halt it completely if you do not continue to work as a result of the urge of procrastination that you feel.

Time is a finite resource to all of us, after all. Each of us only has 24 hours a day to get our job done. How do we spend the time and what are the activities that we do to maximize that valuable resource provided for the benefits of us are entirely up to us as a person. If you choose to spend your time to sleep and do fun activities that are completely unrelated to the work that you need to do to achieve your goals, that is completely up to you although that can slow down the progress to your success as you don't spend the time to accumulate the effort that is needed for success. If you choose to spend your time on the activities that can be done for that, then you can get closer to the things that you want to accomplish in your work.

Therefore, we can say that procrastination hinders our progress because of this limited time factor. You have only a fixed amount of time and you will reduce the ones that you can spend on your progress if you give in to procrastination when you need to choose on how you want to your time.

Moreover, giving in to the urge to procrastinate can actually add up in you too and take a heavy toll on the progress that you need to succeed. When you do it once or twice, it may seem that it does not harm your advancement too much and you can just let it go. But often that kind of thing adds up. It can make you have the habit to give in to procrastination every time because of the enjoyment that you feel when you take that decision. Once that procrastination habit starts to build up, that thing can take a significant amount of your time and slow down your progress to success heavily because you spend more and more time of yours doing the things that give no positive effect for the goals that you want to realize.

That is going to give a bad effect and often it takes a lot of effort to stop the habit once it has rooted itself in your daily rhythm. Procrastination can be highly addictive to us. The longer that you let yourself give in to the desire to procrastinate, the harder it gets for you to not procrastinate in the work that you do.

Because of that, the slowdown effect can build up to your progress to success once you have done it a couple of times regularly. The period and effort that you should have spent in putting in the labor to make you progress faster can instead be used for the things that are completely unrelated to it.

Besides the slowdown of progress that it can cause as described above, that bad effect from procrastination to success can actually be related also to the high possibility of failure that you can have in your chase to success.

Failure Flirt
When you take your time to procrastinate and abandon the work that you need to do, you can make the likelihood of you to meet failure in the road to success bigger. That is because as a result of procrastinating, you can't put in the effort necessary to make the best of your work result. That, in turn, makes the result more prone to being unsatisfactory and below the minimum quality that it should be.

That kind of work result has a bigger chance of meeting failure. When you don't allocate enough time and effort which is needed to get the best result that you can have, then you leave yourself more exposed to mistakes or errors in the work that you do. That causes a bigger probability for things to not go in the way that you want and that can have a direct effect on the accomplishments that you want to achieve by doing the work.

Moreover, there is the cost of opportunity that must be counted as well. An opportunity is usually up for the taking by the people who can come first and take advantage of it as best as it can be taken. By having procrastination go in the way of you to utilize that kind of opportunity that comes in your way, you open more possibility for other people grab that chance first instead of you. That can be another factor that contributes to the failure of your work result besides the not-up-to-standard work results as being described earlier.

Because, when someone is given more amount of time to work on the things that he/she have to, then that person can keep improving it until it can satisfy or even exceed his/her standard. By giving time for procrastination to set in, the time to do that kind of improvement can be reduced significantly and as a result, the improvement that should be done will not be there too and the result can be seen as unsatisfactory even to the person who makes it.

This is not to say that you can avoid failure completely if you don't procrastinate, though. After all, failure is a part and parcel of success and when you try to chase big success, then you are almost guaranteed to have to face some failures along the way that you need to get back from. But we should keep the failure as minimum as possible, of course, because we target success instead of failure. We have to do our best by targeting success in everything that we do even though it is inevitable that we will meet some failures in our pursuit of success. When there is a time when we need to face failures, we should remember to keep getting back up again and maintain our effort to achieve success.

But back to the procrastination matter, if you give in yourself to procrastination most of the time, then you can keep on meeting failure as you don't invest enough time and effort to do your best in your work result. Even if you manage to complete something from your work, there is a big possibility that the quality will not be good as being described earlier as that is not the best effort that you can do in your work.

The often occurrence of failure that can happen as a result of procrastination on your work because of the reasons that are being described above can be bad for your quest to success as you keep having to feel disappointment every time you face the failure. That, in turn, can make you give up easier and quit trying as a result. That is part of explaining why procrastination can lead to quitting besides other important things that should be considered too.

Catalyst of Quitting

Your mental strength probably has its limit. If you have tried and tried again in your pursuit of success but keep on meeting failures, then there is a higher probability that you can say enough to your pursuit and you eventually give up on chasing the success that you want.

When you keep on procrastinating when you do your work, as has been explained in the previous part, you will have a higher possibility of failure and as a result, the chance that you keep on meeting failures is higher too. That can take a toll on you and trigger the urge to quit doing your work.

Even if you don't meet failures that often as a result of your procrastination, trying to get back up from one event of failure needs resolve and work from you too. If you keep on procrastinating in the time that you meet failure when, instead, you need to overcome it and keep on going on your effort to succeed, then it will take a lot of time for you to come back in your work and that is if you want to keep on going despite the failure that you have. If you have a procrastination habit, then you are most likely to quit and give up on the effort when you meet a failure. The reason is because you may think that the time that you need to spend to think of the solution of the failure and implementing it should be spent instead on relaxing and doing other things not related to that. That can be another reason for quitting as a direct result of giving in to the urge of procrastination that comes to you.

And that even assumes that you have put in enough effort to meet the failures that will definitely come in some amount in your road to success. When you have a procrastination preference on all the things that you work on, you may quit when you are in the middle of your effort or even when you just start your journey to pursue success. You see for yourselves how much effort that you need to put in consistently when you are already in the middle of it or just start doing the work. As a result of procrastination, you will not have the resolve needed to continue doing the hard work even further. You can even quit even before you start because of procrastination. If you have an idea or the desire to succeed but then you think about how much effort that is needed from you to go for it until you achieve success, the procrastination preference that you have may take over and as a result, you will decide to *quit on starting* the hard work even before you do start it. That is, of course, a heavy procrastination preference to have and you will have a really small chance of success because of it.

Procrastination can be the catalyst that you need to quit on your pursuit of success and that can happen in all phases of your chase to your achievements. Therefore, you should keep away from it as often as you can because giving in to procrastination can be the main reason why you don't achieve the success that you want. The explanation can be because you are too lazy to do it and it will be such a shame when it comes to that reason. Procrastination, as we have seen, has a very bad relationship with the success that we want.

****

As you have understood from the description above, you should try to diminish your procrastination preference as much as you can if you want to have a high chance of success. The reason is that it can be very detrimental as you will not have enough time and give the effort needed to achieve success.

In the next part, we will begin to define the anti-procrastination mentality that we need in order to remove our procrastination preference and get things done in work. First, we will see what we need to have to build a strong anti-procrastination mentality inside of us. The ones that are needed can be abbreviated as 3Cs and we will see what exactly are those in a deeper discussion in the next chapter.

THE 3CS THAT DEFINE OUR ANTI-PROCRASTINATION MENTALITY

After reading the previous chapter, if you are really serious in working in your best capacity, getting this done, and chasing success, then you will want to have a strong anti-procrastination mentality for yourself.

By having the anti-procrastination mentality, you should be able to dismiss any urge to procrastinate and be lazy that you have in work. Moreover, you can be sure of allocating the best effort as you can be because you focus on your work and not focusing on whether there is a chance for you to relax or wondering what kind of fun activity that you should do with your friends instead when you are immersed with your work.

The anti-procrastination mentality is a powerful thing and you should have one in yourself to utilize the time and effort that you have in the best way that you can for your accomplishments in life.

When you want to avoid procrastination consistently, though, it cannot come instantly in the minute when you want it. You should nurture that kind of mentality bit by bit by always trying your best to avoid spending time doing the things that can be a waste of your working hours. Try to be disciplined in your work and be consistent in putting in the best effort every day in order to build it.

But it can be hard to do, of course, especially when you already get used to procrastinate every time there is something that you have to work on. Just remember when you try to find an excuse to delay or abandon the work that you need to do, doing that can get you further away from having the anti-procrastination mentality that you need to have success with. Instead, you will nurture a pro-procrastination mentality that slows down the progress in your work significantly. That is not good and as you keep yourself being led to relax and do wasting time activities, the time that you can spend on your actual work keeps on decreasing.

Hence, anti-procrastination mentality can be one of the most important factors that you can have in your work. By having a strong one, you can be sure that you work to the best of your ability and keep on having the motivation to do your job consistently in the time that is allocated for work.

And that is needed if you want to have success. After all, only consistent effort in a period of time can lead you to accomplish what you want to. The more you give yourself in procrastination, the less chance you have to work constantly as you need.

The anti-procrastination mentality is something that you need to keep on building in the fastest way that you can to achieve success in your work and getting things done.

Now that you know better about the importance of anti-procrastination mentality to the work that we do, you may want to understand: what are the things that define that kind of mentality? There can be several factors but here, I give a highlight to the three things that can be of the most important things that shape it which can be abbreviated to 3 Cs. They are our cause, consistency, and continuation. Having each of these should greatly help you in terms of trying to avoid procrastination as often as possible.

The Cause

When you think of the time that you spend by giving in to procrastination, try to reflect: what is the real reason of your decision at that time to choose to abandon your work for relaxing and doing other things that are unrelated to your work?

Can it be because the objective of the work is not that important to you? That its purpose is not too crucial for you so you can readily ditch it for the other activities that are more enjoyable?

If your work objective is something meaningful to you, then it should be easier for you not to procrastinate and have the barrier of procrastination ready for your work. It is because you are going to have the needed motivation to continue your hard work at that time to chase what you want as achieving that can mean the world to you. Relaxing and doing other things that can take the time needed for the work should be a second priority for you as a result of that.

As you can probably see from the description above, the reason why you do things can be a powerful thing that defines the strength of your anti-procrastination mentality. The cause, the first of the C from the 3 Cs that define anti-procrastination mentality, is something that you need to think about.

What is the purpose that you have by doing the work that you do? What is the objective that makes you need to put in the effort every day?

If you can answer that convincingly for you and are able to muster things that have a strong meaning to you, then you will have it easier to make your anti-procrastination mentality stronger.

The motivation and eagerness that you have to do something are completely related to the things that make you do it.

When you have a weak cause to do your activities, then it will be much harder for you to keep on working when the urge to procrastinate comes in. You will have weaker reasons to stay in your course and maintain your work as you come to that kind of situation at some point of your work.

And as a result, you will delay or abandon your work instead to do other things. That, of course, cannot be good if you want to achieve your success as soon as possible.

But then again, the success that you have defined can be unimportant for you so that you do not have the motivation to fight the urge of procrastination that comes to you at your work.

As you think more about it, the causal factor in the anti-procrastination mentality has some other importance to avoid procrastination besides the ones that have been explained above:

- A strong cause can give the inspiration that you need to solve the problems and struggles which you face in your road to success instead of feeling down and stop doing the hard work as a result of giving in to procrastination
- A strong cause can give you the push to add the extra miles in your work by spending the time that is actually outside of your working hours. The time that can actually be spent to do nothing will be utilized to work on the things that can bring you closer to success
- A strong cause can serve as an additional motivation that you can look into whenever you need to ask yourself why you need to do the thing which is related to your work. You can answer the question by saying you need to do it to achieve the success that you want because you have a strong cause

When you have something that is worth it to be pursued by doing the work that you need to do, it can become the deflection that you need to the urge for procrastination that you feel. By remembering the cause which becomes the main reason to work hard on something, that can be the motivation and the base for the anti-procrastination mentality that you need to maintain the commitment of putting in the effort in the schedule of your work hours.

The Consistency

When you need to fight the desire to procrastinate in your work time, one of the things that you should have is the consistency in the work that you do.

By having consistency in your labor, you should have additional support in not giving way for the laziness to come into your mind. That is because you have the resolve to keep on going to do your job in the working hours and that should help you to leave no room for any other activities which have no significance to it.

The discipline in consistency, however, is something that you must build. It can be pretty hard at the start as you do not get used to the constant work that you need to do in a set of time. But as time goes by and you have got more of the rhythm of the activity that you need to do, it should get easier and easier for you to build the work consistency in every day.

Then, when you finally have a high degree of consistency, relaxing and doing fun activities aside from your work should be able to be easily put out of your mind in the time that you need to work. After all, you already have a clear and fix guidance in your head when you need to work and when you have the time to relax. Because of the consistency that you have trained step-by-step, you should be able to decide firmly for yourself that you need to work at this time of the day and not wavered by the thoughts of resting and enjoying other things as often becomes the case for you when you suddenly have the urge for procrastination.

Looking at the explanation above, consistency becomes a strong weapon that you can use to fight laziness. Thus, that is one characteristic that makes itself as one important thing to have when you want to build a strong anti-procrastination mentality.

Besides fighting off laziness that can occasionally occur to us, consistency is needed so that we can keep on going with our work despite the boring feeling that we feel to our activities or the uncertainty that we face as a result of the fruits from our labor that have not come to us. As we probably know, when we try to work on something for so long and we still wait for the success that we want to come to us as a result of our work, we can feel bored and insecure that is caused by the work that we have to do every day. This can trigger inside of us the urge of procrastination as well as we try to not to give up despite the circumstances that we feel does not support our work. By trying to stick to the work consistency that we have built all this time, we can avoid the trap of giving in to procrastination at trying times like these as we try to not stop working until we reach the results that we want. Having work consistency can help to make sure that we keep on working and strengthen our anti-procrastination mentality significantly despite the feeling that we have.

After all, procrastination can come in various ways that can distract our rhythm in work. Laziness, boredness, despair for results, feeling that what we work on is not worth our time, seeing other people relaxing and enjoying their time, and some other reasons can be the trigger for us to delay or abandon our work and relax or do other things instead. If you have not built your pattern of work and stay strong into it, then it will be easy for procrastination to get you and make you stop doing the work that you currently do. There are many causes of procrastination that can come to our way and having consistency in the work that we do can help us tremendously in keeping up the pace in terms of putting in the effort every time.

Consistency is something that you have to build also from time to time in our work. Strong consistency in the things that we do should be able to support our anti-procrastination mentality significantly besides the cause that we have and the continuation which will be explained deeper after this.

The Continuation
When we try to do our work, failure or any other problems can come to our way and can make us have stronger preference to procrastinate because we feel that what we have worked on until this point is not enough. We can feel that probably we don't have the right ability to be able to constantly do the work in the things that we need to do.

Problems and struggles can really test our immunity to procrastination. After all, when you experience them in your work, if you don't try to overcome it, then it will become the roadblock that makes you lazy and lose the motivation to go back and keep on working. Those things can create a strong urge to procrastinate to us as we think that we better do the other things that are more enjoyable than doing the work that make us meet troubles and seems hard for us to solve them.

And, when you think about it, that is one of the reasons why we have procrastination for the first time. As being told in the previous chapter of this book, our mind always wants to have something simpler and not risky. By facing the troubles and problems that we have in our work, we trigger our instinct to just abandon the work that is complicated and seems to have full of problems. Then, we switch our attention to the activities that are simpler and more enjoyable to us like relaxing or doing fun activities together with our friends.

It is in that moment when you can count on the strength of the continuity mindset that you have. By having this part of the 3Cs, you can be surer that you are going to keep on going and try to overcome the struggles that you have met in your work rather than giving up and stop working.

After all, struggles like that usually come often if we do something daily and we keep on doing our job for a long time. Each problem usually comes with its uniqueness too in terms of the situation compared to the ones that we may have faced. If we don't have the continuation mindset inside of us, then we should be ready to give in to the urge of procrastination that we have in our minds. That is because we don't have the drive to keep on going after we have been halted by the problems that we meet and this kind of situation that we are in surely makes a strong temptation to each and every one of us to procrastinate.

I mean, there is no problem that is associated with relaxing activities and if we go back to work, then we will have to face the same problems again before we can move on from that. Sometimes, that can be an easy choice for each of us whether we prefer to relax or to work in the trying times, right?

That is why, if you want to keep on working and fight the urge of procrastination during your setbacks, then you need to have a continuation mindset in you. That thing is going to help you build a strong anti-procrastination mentality as well. It can be hard to do that, understandably, but you have to keep on working so you can achieve the results that you want from it.

Difficult times can be annoying and can make you lose your motivation in terms of working. When you are in this kind of situation, then you should always remember to have your continuation with you and keep on working despite the problems that you have because only by then that you can solve them and move on to the success that you want in work.

****

So, you have seen a detailed explanation about the 3Cs that can help to define the strong anti-procrastination mentality that you want to have and how each of them contributes to this mentality that we try to build. What are the things that you can do, though, to help growing each of them in your work so you are more immune to the urge of procrastination?

In the next chapters, we are going to see what we can do for that using three pillars that can shape each of the 3Cs. The three pillars are motivation, habit, and focus. Each of the pillars can contribute to help you in having a strong 3Cs and eventually a powerful anti-procrastination mentality. We will take a deeper look at them in the following chapter.

THREE ANTI-PROCRASTINATION MENTALITY PILLARS: MOTIVATION, HABIT, FOCUS

Now that you have known what are the things that constitute an anti-procrastination mentality, it is the time to learn how to build that mentality based on that.

When you just start working and don't have the right discipline to fight the urge of procrastination within you, then it will be easy for you to fall victim to the other activities which seem more enjoyable then your work. After all, the happy feeling that you get when you procrastinate can be much more alluring compared to the stress that you may have to face when you do your work.

Only by consciously trying to prevent yourself to delay or abandon your work in the working hours again and again, then you will begin to shape the anti-procrastination mentality for yourself and be more adept to keep on working. That way, you can become a significantly more productive person and can optimize more of the time that you have to do something meaningful for yourself or other people around you.

That kind of discipline can be and should be built by you if you want to seriously get the best result that you can have from your work. By having the resolve to put aside the desire for procrastination that you have in mind during the work that you do, then you should be able to put in more consistent effort and time for the work that you do. That can be crucial in shaping your work result to be the best as it can be.

When you try to see what you can do to build a strong anti-procrastination mentality in you, then there are many things that you can do to shape that kind of mentality. It can be simplified by trying to build the 3 Cs that have been described earlier and getting the discipline that you need to be able to work optimally. The things to shape a strong anti-procrastination mentality that we are going to focus on here are the three pillars that can be the most important to note in terms of trying to build a strong anti-procrastination mentality. They can be helped to grow in order to make your barrier to procrastination stronger.

The three pillars of anti-procrastination mentality are: motivation, habit, and focus.

When we talk about motivation and its relation to the work and procrastination that we must fight to stay away from, then there is a clear reason why it is important. Motivation is what drives you to work and having it in a strong form, stronger than the preference that you have in regards to procrastination, will be one of the keys for you to build your anti-procrastination mentality that comes from the cause, consistency, and continuity that you have in you.

If you want this motivation pillar to be able to help you in terms of fighting procrastination, then you should source and maintain a strong motivation for your work. You should try to figure out how to have a meaningful one initially before you decide to work on things, maintain it during the course of your work, and keep it strong even when you face some problems and struggles in the work that you do.

That is related to the cause, consistency, and continuation that you should have in the build-up of the anti-procrastination mentality. How you shape your motivation is important to strengthen each of them in yourself.

There is also the habit pillar. When you work on something that you need to do, then it is down to you to develop positive habits that can help to support your work and keep you away from the urge of procrastination that may come up in the work process. That positive habit should be shaped by the things that you do consciously to make your work more optimized and make your work protected from the laziness that might be triggered when it comes to the time that you have to work hard consistently.

If you try to build good habits that can contribute significantly to the anti-procrastination mentality that you want to have, then you need to identify first what kind of habit that you should have to do that. Here, we suggest some positive habits that can help you in terms of maintaining or even improving the work process that you have while keeping you away from giving in to the urge of procrastination that you have in work. I hope each of the habits can be implemented to help you to do your work in the best way that you can.

The positive habits that you want to have in your work, though, must also be consistently nurtured every day so you can get used to it and can utilize it optimally to help in the work result that you want. Hence, you must try to implement the things that you consider as a good habit immediately and do it every time so it can support you more in optimizing your work and keeping you away from procrastination. See how the good habits go so you know that they can really help you in terms of having an anti-procrastination mentality

Last but not least, the focus is another thing that we are going to talk about more deeply here to help you shape your anti-procrastination mentality. When you have a strong focus on your work, then you should be able to repel any thinking of procrastination that may come to your mind during the course of your work. Focus can guide you too in terms of narrowing your effort to the things that can be the most beneficial for you to work with so you can get the most results from the effort and time that you have put in.

When you try to implement focus to the cause, consistency, and continuation that help to define our strong anti-procrastination mentality, then you must be ready to divert your attention fully to the things that have the most meaning to your work or can contribute most heavily to the success of your work results. If it means that you should work harder on fewer things than before and give up on the things that can prevent you to work optimally on those fewer things, then you should do that when that means you can have a greater chance to have better results from the works that you do.

Motivation, habit, and focus can combine to help you strengthen your 3 Cs that define a strong anti-procrastination mentality. By having the right ones for the pillars all together, then you can work without having to worry too much about the urge of procrastination because you already have strong support that can help you in fighting with that kind of thinking. One should note though that motivation, habit, and focus can be different to each of us when it comes to defining what are the right ones for them in our work. The things that are given in the next parts of this book are somethings that should be adapted to each of your personal condition at work. By thinking through them and having them as the right ones for you and your work, then it should be optimized to support your work effort as to keep away from procrastination. That can be the greatest thing that you can do to have a strong anti-procrastination mentality in your work.

As you have previously seen in the book structure given in the early part of the book, each of the pillars will be explained in terms of how it can support each of the Cs in a strong anti-procrastination mentality. This is done to make them more focused in helping you to build each component of the mentality. This optimization is hoped can be useful for you to have a strong mentality in fighting the urge of procrastination.

Without further ado, let's get to the first part that we will discuss, the Motivation pillar help for the first part of the 3 Cs, Cause.

MOTIVATION BUILD 1 – CAUSE: GET THE POWERFUL TARGETS

If you have read my previous book about working in the passion that you have, then you have known quite well about the importance of the targets that you have for the motivation in your work.

Targets are the reason of why you work. They are the why that supports your how. When you don't have a powerful target that can give you a strong motivation to continue with your work, then it will be easier for you to give in to the urge of procrastination that may come in during the course of your work. That is because you don't have enough push to keep working on the things that you do. You don't have enough reason to prioritize it to the relaxation and other fun activities that you might be able to do in your time.

Hence, that is the main reason why you should get powerful targets for the things that you do. Having them can be your strong source of cause to keep on working and ignoring the call to relax that you may have in your mind during your work. Achieving those goals, after all, is stronger call for you than when you compare it to the benefits that can be had by giving in to the procrastination activities.

Having powerful targets can also help you related to your fight with procrastination in terms of giving you the drive that you need to always be motivated to give the extra efforts that are sometimes needed at work. When you work on something, there can be times when you need to put on that little bit of extra work after the regular work that you have done to make the results better and the impact of your work can be more felt by people. By having powerful targets that can be helped to be achieved by the extra effort that you give, you will be more eager to get the job done and put off the feeling to relax after the normal hours of your work if it means that it can get you closer to realize the targets that you have in your work.

There are many things that can be had by setting powerful targets for your work in building your motivation and aiding the cause in your anti-procrastination mentality. But how can you think of the powerful targets that can make you work like that?

When you try to see what are the powerful targets that can be set for the cause of your anti-procrastination mentality, you should take a look at what is the thing that can be the most meaningful aspect to you in life. Is it financial? Is it social? Is it influence? That way you can have the start that you might need in thinking of the targets that should be the objective of your work. That can also be one of the considerations for you to evaluate whether the goals that you currently have for your work is strong enough or not.

What are the other things that you must consider when you try to get some powerful targets to support your anti-procrastination campaign? There are three things which I suggest here: question the push that you get from the targets, make the prioritization of the targets that you want to achieve in your work, and think about the people close to you when you set the goals that can have a strong meaning for you so you can ditch that urge of procrastination during your work. We will take a closer look at the following parts on how you can do them.

Question the Push

Think about the work that you do daily and the objectives that you may have in doing that kind of work consistently. How do the objectives motivate you in giving everything that you have got for the success of the work? Do you consider delaying or abandoning the work that you do when you remember the purpose of your work or do you feel more motivated to work harder and ignore the calls of relaxing when you recall why you do the work?

Well, I hope that you get more energy to work by answering those questions in your mind and feel the strong motivation flowing through you as you remember the targets that you have in doing the work that you do. That means that you have found some targets that are worth it for you to pursue and they have the necessary push that can help you to build a strong cause in the anti-procrastination mentality that you want when you read this book.

If you don't, well then you have to reconsider the targets that you want to achieve in your work. You might even want to reconsider the work that you do if it is closely related to your targets as there is a high probability for you to not do your best and procrastinate in work when you have the chance to do so.

Powerful targets that contribute to the cause of anti-procrastination mentality should give you the push that is needed to keep on working. When you think that you don't feel enough motivation to work hard on your job when you take a look at its objectives, then it means that the targets that you have currently are not powerful enough to fight the procrastination that you may occasionally have while doing your work.

In terms of deciding whether the targets that you have set is powerful enough to avoid your laziness, here are some other questions that can be your pointer in doing that:

- Are the targets that you have related to the aspects of life that you think are important and should be prioritized?
- Imagine that you have accomplished the targets as a result of your work. What do you feel when you do that? Do you feel happy, proud, or it is just a so and so feeling that you have?
- Do you feel motivated when you get up every day having to do your work to achieve those targets?
- When you think about your objectives, are there any other targets that come to your mind as somethings should be worked on more instead of the current ones that you have?
- If those current targets that you have for work on are the things that you need to chase for most of your life, what do you feel about that?
- Are you and/or the people close to you in a presumably better condition if you eventually achieve those targets for your work?
- When you compare the targets to the work that is expected to be done if you want to achieve them, what is your feeling? Do you think it is worth it to keep going to achieve those targets if you have to work with that way?
- If you know that you cannot fail in your effort for everything, then do you still consider to work to succeed achieving those targets?

If you answer positively to the preference of your targets in most of the questions, then consider yourself having the right push from the targets that you chase in your work. That way you should have the goals that can contribute themselves to the cause of a strong anti-procrastination mentality that you want.

If you don't, however, then you have to think other targets that you can have that can answer most of the questions above positively. That is needed so you can make them a strong source of motivation in your work to avoid procrastination.

The push that you have from your targets should be one of the most important things to keep you work hard in the things that you need to do.

Make Targets Prioritization

There can be a number of targets that you want to achieve by doing your work. To have the most powerful ones show themselves up and become the source of motivation that you need to avoid procrastination, then you can do worse than having prioritization on them to have it sorted out.

When you work on something consistently, most likely there are some targets, personal or professional, that can be realized if you keep constant hard work on it. For example, if you work in your job in the marketing division of a company, there can be some objectives that you want to realize. Probably to make a product achieve brand recognition in the region where it is sold by more than 50%, maintain existing product popularity, or maybe there are some personal targets too related to your job like promoting yourself to become the Vice President of Marketing in the company.

There can be many targets that are associated with the work that you do. Some of them are more important than others for you personally. Therefore, to make them more helpful for you to build a strong cause in the anti-procrastination mentality, you can try to formulate the prioritization of the targets that you have in your work.

Targets' prioritization can help in avoiding procrastination in some ways. By making prioritization to the objectives that you have, you can understand what are the things that are actually more important to you when you do the work. That way, you can direct your work to the things that have more meaning to you and that can give you more motivation to keep on going with your work instead of procrastinating.

Doing that can also make some targets which can be invincible for you in the days that you work but actually related to it to show themselves up. Those targets might be something that you consider as powerful targets too for your work but you do not realize them. That can happen because when you need to prioritize your targets, then you will think of any target which is associated and can be done with the work that you do. Because of that, you can have some additional motivation to work by knowing that producing an excellent result in it will bring you closer to achieve those targets. Thus, the chance of you to procrastinate will be less likely too because of the added motivation.

Target prioritization can also help you in determining whether the targets that are associated with your work should be worth it to chase. This might be related to the push of the targets which have been discussed in the previous part. If you don't think that the targets that should be prioritized are important for you, then you are most likely to procrastinate given the chance. This also might explain why you often procrastinate in the past in your work if you happen to do that. When you do, it might be better to consider changing the work that you do every day in order to have new targets to look out to that are more meaningful to you.

When you do prioritization to the targets associated with your work, you can do some tips which are given below:

- Try to completely list all the targets that can be associated with the work that you do. There may be some which are not too visible but can be important to you if you make it as a target. For example, when you work for your business, then there may some effects of the products that you produce that can be associated with making the social welfare better for some people that are affected by it and you might not realize it until you think about the goals that can be associated with your work in this target prioritization activity

- Ask the questions which are given regarding the push that you get from each of the targets to help you in determining whether it is important to you and it should get top prioritization for you to chase in your work. The benefit of targets in terms of building an anti-procrastination mentality is to help you get the motivation to keep on working and abandoning the thought of relaxing in your working hours. Understanding the push that you get from those targets in the prioritization activity will help you to achieve that benefit more

- If you have trouble in terms of giving prioritization ranks to the targets directly or you want a clearer assessment in the process, then maybe you need a previous step by thinking of the variables that should be used in the prioritization related to the importance of the targets and the weight for each of the variables based on its meaning to you. After that, you can assess each of the targets quantitatively by giving scores (probably from 1-10) to each of them in terms of how you see it on each of the important variables that you have. After that, you can multiply the scores by the weight of the variables to get the total score of importance for the targets. That will be the basis of your prioritization

Making the right prioritization can be crucial to the cause aspect of your anti-procrastination mentality. Because by doing that, you will know more about the powerful targets that you can achieve by working your jobs and as a result, you have more power to avoid procrastination.

Think About Everyone
The thing that is the most important to you can be not yourself but the people that you love or maybe other people that are close to you. Therefore, the most powerful target that you can associate with your work can be not related to yourself but the welfare of the people that you most care about.

When you try to think about the powerful targets that can help you in terms of building a strong cause for your anti-procrastination mentality, then you can also think about the association of your work result with people other than yourself. For this, you can ask to yourself: who are the people that you care about? What are the things that can be resulted from the impact of your work that can be associated with them too? By doing your work in the best way that you can and producing excellent work results from it, can you give something which is meaningful to them?

If you think about your targets this way, then it can be possible that the most powerful targets for you are actually more related to those people around you. By knowing that, you can set the targets which are more meaningful to you. They might not directly impact you but they can have the most importance to you.

After all, if you think only about yourself when you set your work targets, then it might not be as motivating as when you see them in terms of its impact on the other people. When you have targets that are related to other people, then you might have more reasons to stop procrastinating and keep on working because the result will not only affect you but the people that you care about too.

And it actually does not stop just for the people in the circle of your friends or families. When the work that you do can directly or indirectly impact other people in the society, then that can also be the powerful targets that you need for building up a strong anti-procrastination mentality if you care about that. That kind of social impact is also able to give you a strong motivation for your work as long as you give strong attention to that aspect personally.

The attention to other people in your work can be the strong motivation that you also need to further fuel your work and give you the protection you need in work from the urge of procrastination. The targets that affect other people who you love may be the most powerful target that you can have to put in your optimal work.

****

As we have learned, powerful targets to trigger your motivation and shape the cause aspect in your anti-procrastination mentality can be one of the most important things to have. There are things that you can do to set powerful targets related to your work. As being explained previously, some of them are thinking of the push that you get from the targets, doing targets prioritization, and thinking about the targets that are related to other people.

Next, to further strengthen your motivation pillar to shield yourself more from procrastination, we will take a look at how the pillar can be implemented to support another C in the anti-procrastination mentality, which is Consistency.

MOTIVATION BUILD 2 – CONSISTENCY: OPTIMIZE YOUR WORK CONTEXT

The right work environment can be another thing that serves as additional motivation and supports your work consistency too while also give the push to avoid the urge of procrastination that can occasionally come to your work.

As a worker, we can have our preference that is different to other people in terms of the work environment that can optimize our work process and make us feel comfortable to constantly put in the best effort in our job. Having the right set of it can make us work to our maximum and motivate us to keep working despite the laziness or boredness that we might feel in relation to our work. Likewise, working in the wrong environment that is not our preference can decrease our motivation and as a result, we will be more prone to abandon or delay the work that we do when we have the chance for it.

Trying to have a work environment according to our preference can be a daunting task, though. When we work for ourselves, then probably it will be much easier for us to change our work environment as it is completely up to us to determine where or when we work. We can work at home in the night if we prefer and there will be little to no objection to it from other people. When we work for other people, though, then it will be more difficult as we are probably required to go to the office to do our work. To mitigate that, then you can try to come to the people who are related to the decision to show how working in the environment that you prefer can boost your productivity, your work result, and your contribution to the company that you work in. If the other people think what you offer makes sense and can benefit the company, then it will be easier for them to let you do your work according to your preference. This can depend on the job position that you hold, though, as if you work for a position that requires you to be in your place in the office all the time, then you probably cannot change the setting to your desire. There are other aspects that you can work on and there could also be some solutions that can satisfy the requirement of your workplace and your preference. That should be your focus in terms of setting the optimum work environment.

As for the additional motivation that can be given by the preferred work environment, it can only be right as the reason we try to set the work context that we have into our desire. After all, there should be nothing wrong in trying to give additional help to the work that we do so we can produce the best results from it and can have some more motivation in doing it while building the consistency part in our anti-procrastination mentality to be stronger to resist the halt that can come from the urge of procrastination.

When it comes to optimize your work context, there are some things that we can do to formulate it. Work context is related to the place, the time, and the facilities that we have to practice the preferable methods for our work. The place and the facilities related to our preference can be set beforehand and we can try to always work in their settings that we prefer. The time, on the other hand, is something that we should practice to do every day in order to have our work done mostly in the period that we desire. We will discuss in deep about what we can do for each of them in the following part.

Adjust the Workplace

The place where we do our work can be important in terms of setting the mood for your work consistency.

The settings of this can vary too in terms of the scope. It can be related to the where is the location that you do your work. Some people prefer to work in a place where there are a lot of people such as in a café or mall while other people prefer to work in office settings. There can be others too who prefer quiet places such as in their home or other places where they can be alone to fully concentrate on the jobs that they do.

The settings for your preferred place can also be more detailed too and it can be related to the preferred adjustment of things around where the person work. For example, some people may prefer that the table where they work on is clean and only consists of the equipment and tools that will be used in the work that they do. Others may feel that some snacks and drinks will be good in terms of the things that should be placed close to them in work and they may want their table to be a little bit messy in order to get the ideas for their work flow easier.

It is completely up to the person who knows his/her exact taste on what kind of place that can maximize the output of his/her work. Everyone can have a different preference and distinct desire when it comes to designing the location where they can work with more motivation.

One thing that we should pay attention to that can have a strong relationship with our preferred workplace is our personality. If you are an extrovert who prefers to have people around you, then maybe it is better if you can work in a place where there are many people that can "accompany" you in your work and where you can meet many new people. On the other hand, if you are an introvert, then probably you prefer a place where you can work on your own and have a quiet environment to it. That is because you most likely cannot concentrate on the work if you are surrounded by many people and meet with others during your work.

That personality can also be on whether you are a more creative or analytical person. If you are a creative one, then maybe you prefer your place to work to be messier and fuller of things that can inspire you to have new ideas or provoke your thoughts to think about something that is related to your work. If you are an analytical person, though, then you probably prefer to have it neat around in your workplace and you want to have tools around you that can help you in doing the analysis that you need in your work.

There can be variations to it and it should be up to you to determine what kind of workplace can optimally motivate your work consistency.

By finding the optimal workplace that you can work on and do your work in that place you preferred, you are likely to love doing your work more and build on the consistency part of your anti-procrastination mentality every day you work in your preferred place.

When trying to define the optimal workplace where you can do your job, there are some things that you can do:
- Try to take a personality test to know more about it. There are some excellent tests that you can take to understand deeper about your personalities such as Myers-Briggs Type Indicator (MBTI) or Dominance, Influence Steadiness, and Compliance (DISC). Doing this may make you know better about what kind of place that you prefer based on your personality

- Try to remember the experience that you get from where you work before. You probably have worked on some different settings before. Take a note on the details of the place that you find most comfortable and stimulating for you to do your work

- Test the settings in the place. Try some different details in the location that you work for some period of time, for example, a week for each setting, and see where is the best place that you can produce your best work

By implementing those points, you should be able to find a place where you are the most comfortable in terms of working. By having that kind of knowledge, it should help you optimize your work context in terms of place and from there, you should be able to work with more motivation and able to repel the urge of procrastination with more power.

Understand Your Optimal Time
Besides the place where you work, you can also consider having the advantage of time preference as the additional motivation on the things that you need to do as well.

People have a different preference in terms of time in which they work as in the case of the workplace earlier. There are people who seem to have more concentration if they work in the morning and some other people prefer to work to their fullest in the night. This is related to the work rhythm that you have in a day and working in your most likable period of the day can boost the mood that you need for work significantly.

When you try to identify the time when you are most inspired to do the work to take the advantage of additional motivation from it, try to consider the complication of the situation in which can happen if you work during that preferred time of the day. If, for example, you see that you work most optimally in the night but the office where you work in is already closed in that period of the day, then maybe you can consider working in night in your home when you have the time and therefore, you have less work to do in the morning or in the other period of the day when you are less optimized to work.

By having the knowledge of your optimal time to work, then you can optimize that period of time in the day to get most of your job done. Hence, you can maximize your output by allocating some of your work that requires more of your attention in the time of the day where you have the most motivation to do the job. Being able to do so can also boost the consistency of your work and help you to avoid procrastination by allocating the other period of your day when you don't need to work for the relaxing and doing some other fun activities that you want to do.

However, for sure, you must also think about when the work *should* be done and whether working in the period of time that you prefer can have a bad effect for you. If you have a deadline that you cannot negotiate in that day or if you have some works which you have to discuss with your colleagues in another period of the day besides your preferred window of time, then, of course, you have to adapt your work to that requirement too and do as best as you can to your work during that time. Only when the circumstances allow should you consider to allocate most of your work to be done in the time when you prefer to do it.

But when you have the opportunity to do work in the time that you prefer consistently, then you should adapt your working hours so you should be able to do it. By adapting your working hours and your relaxing hours to your preference, you should be able to be more consistent in work and can push aside the possibility that you will give in to the procrastination during that preferred work hours. That is because you have committed yourself to work during that time of yours and you should also have more motivation to do your work in that period.

Practice the Preferable Method

The third thing that you can optimize in your work context is the facilities or tools that you have to make you able to do the things that you need in your work in the way that you prefer.

As a worker, you might have the desire to optimize your work process and result by having the things that are able to support you for that. For example, if you work in something that requires you to cook some food, then you should surround your work environment with the tools that make you able to do the things that are needed to produce the optimum version of food that you can cook. By doing that, you should be able to improve your consistency in work because you feel more motivated to do it with the facilities that you have as they can support you to do your job optimally.

Besides the tools that you need to optimize, you can also think about the methods that you apply to approach the job that you have. Probably, in the work that you do, you prefer to do it by having a discussion first regarding what you need to work on before you begin to implement the discussion result in your task. If you feel that you have a more optimized work process by doing it that way and that is the method that you prefer to do your work, then you should try to do it if it is possible as it can help your motivation in work too. It also can make you avoid procrastination that can be triggered by doing your work in the method that you less prefer.

When you try to optimize your approach to do your work, use the tools that you need in the work environment to optimize your work process, and have more consistency to do your work while building the anti-procrastination mentality as a result of having work context more optimized, there are things that you might want to consider to do:

- Compare the budget with the advantages that you get for the facilities and tools that you need to work optimally. While it may be nice to have all of the best tools and facilities that you want in place and ready for you to use for work, that might be not become nice when you look into the budget that you have for that kind of facility or tool. Try to compare between the budget and the advantage that you can get using the facility or tool. If it is not too far in terms of the function, probably you can use the ones that you already have or buy the facility or tool that is cheaper to help you in work

- Keep trying to update your approach to work to the newest ones and see the effect. The world keeps changing and there may be new methods found that can be used to make your work more effective. It can be to your advantage if you try the new methods that you have noticed and see whether it fits you while bringing better results for your work. If it is, then you will have a new method to prefer to use with the better results from your work as a result to boot

- Benchmark the tools/facilities and the approach that you use with other people in the same work as you. This process can probably give you some inspiration in terms of the best and preferred tools/facilities and approach to use. Often, you can find that those things that the other people use may be more to your liking too than the ones that you have already utilized currently in your work process

By trying to optimize what you have in terms of facilities or tools around you and the approach that you have to work to the ones that you prefer and those that bring better results for you, you should see more results from your work and you should also be able to do your job for more consistency to shape your anti-procrastination mentality even more.

****

As you have already learned from above, optimizing your work context can bring significant results to your work consistency and get you additional motivation that you might need because your preferred way to do your work has been fulfilled. Preferred place, time, and method that are being set to your work should help to avoid giving in to the procrastination feeling that you may have during your work.

In the next part, we will take a look at how to build your motivation pillar so it can help you too in the continuation aspect in strong anti-procrastination mentality that you want to have. The method that we will suggest here is comparison which will give the motivation that you might need to keep on going despite meeting some problems on your work, although you have to be careful with your perspective when doing the comparison to not let that process demotivates you instead.

MOTIVATION BUILD 3 – CONTINUATION: COMPARE CURRENT CONDITION

Now, comparing your current condition with the others may have a positive or negative effect on your anti-procrastination mentality. That is one thing that should be noted and remembered.

There is a saying that tells us you should not compare your situation with anyone as each person has a different path in his/her life. That can be true if you, for example, do the comparison to your more successful friend, then you feel down and think that you don't have the same potential with your friend. As a result, you think that there is nothing that you can change in your condition. That is the kind of reaction from the comparison process which will cause a negative effect to your anti-procrastination mentality as your motivation to work hard will then be reduced. You think that however hard you may work, you won't be able to have the success that your friend currently has.

Well, that is the negative effect but it can also have a positive effect on your motivation for the anti-procrastination mentality that you want to have. It is just a matter of changing your perspective to the comparison result.

I mean, what if instead you feel down as you don't think that you can match your friend's achievement because you don't have it inside of you to do it, you change the way you see it to something else: that you need to work even harder so you are able to have the kind of success that your friend has accomplished too? Your friend must have done his/her share of hard work as there is no success that can be gained without high amount of effort for some period and because of that, he/she can get to the position where he/she is currently. If you keep on putting in the effort and work even harder than your friend to something that you want to achieve, then you may be able to match that success of your friend or even exceed it.

That is the kind of mentality that you should have and that is the kind of perspective which will be able to help you to build your anti-procrastination mentality from the comparison process as you feel that you will be more left behind by your friend if you give in to the urge of procrastination that you have during your work. A change of perspective can help you to see things in significantly more beneficial way for you.

That is what I mean too when I say that you should benefit by comparing your current condition with other people who have achieved more success than you in relation to shaping the continuation aspect of your anti-procrastination mentality. When you face with problems when working in something, then the comparison that you do can bring the motivation to keep on working by thinking that if you don't do anything to bring you back to the position of being able to work without the problems, then it will be much longer for you to find the success that you want.

Hard work can bring the solution that you need to the problems that you meet at work. That is only if you are serious in working and not just surrender yourself to the procrastination urge that can get stronger if you meet some problems at work.

Regarding the comparison that you can do to make you feel more motivated to work hard and forget procrastination, you can do that by comparing yourself to the person that you imagine that you can be, a member of your friends or families, or with the successful people that do the same work as you. We will discuss more next to how each of them can bring the motivation in you to keep working and distance yourself from procrastination.

Compare with Your Ideal Self

There must be some version of you that you aspire yourself to be in your work, right?

For example, if you work in the division of HR in a company, then probably you want yourself to be the expert of HR that can lead your company in that area. If you work in your own business, then you probably have the desire to be the most successful person in the industry that you are in.

It is very normal for every person to have an ideal self in the field that he/she works in. That kind of thing is good as long as you use it to motivate yourself so you eventually be able to realize that version of you.

When you compare yourself currently with the person that you think as an ideal version of yourself, what do you see? How far are you in terms of gap between the current and the ideal version of you? More importantly, what can you do at the moment so you can bridge that gap in relation to your work as fast as possible?

If you are in work and have the feeling to procrastinate, then you should feel more motivated to work by thinking on the answers of those questions because you want to be the person that you dream of as soon as you can and the only way you can do that is by working in the time that you have optimally.

When it comes to the problems that you face in your work that makes you want to delay or abandon the work that you do, there is a strong possibility that you will feel motivated to solve the problems instead of stopping by thinking about the comparison. It is because if you don't overcome the problems that you have currently, then it will be very hard for you to keep on going to achieve the ideal version of yourself in the work that you do.

That kind of push can be crucial in terms of building the continuation aspect that you need for a strong anti-procrastination mentality. By knowing that only by putting in the effort continuously can help you to realize that target of yours at work, then you can keep on working instead of procrastinating and do nothing.

When you think about the comparison of yourself with the person that you want to be, doing the things below can help you to build the continuation aspect in your anti-procrastination mentality:

- Think and formulate about the most effective way that you can work to be faster in achieving the ideal version of you. Is there anything in your approach to work currently that you should change in regards to that?
- When you meet problems in work, think of them as some challenges that you need to overcome to prove yourself worthy to become the ideal version of yourself
- If the ideal version of you meet the problems like the ones that you face currently, then what will he/she do? Imagining that might help you in solving the problems that you have in your work in the best way
- Learn skills or approaches that your future ideal self might have which can be used to solve the problems. You might be lacking in ability to overcome the problems in your work currently but that should not stop you to try to learn what skills that your ideal self might have which can be used to do it

- Test and trial. The problems will not be solved on its own and you need to implement the ideas of solving it that you might have in your mind to see whether it will work or not. Think about it as yet another effort that you can do to learn and improve yourself more from experience as you aim to realize your ideal self-version

The comparison with the person that you want to be in the future in the area of your work should be able to motivate you to overcome the problems that you have. Using that kind of motivation, you can build the continuation aspect of your anti-procrastination mentality positively.

Compare with Your Peers

As people who work to achieve the success that we want, sometimes we compare ourselves with how our families or friends do in terms of their progress to success. This is true especially in the modern era where there is a technology like social media that makes it much easier for us to see how do other people do in their work and life.

When we do that kind of comparison and we see that some of them are more successful than us, it should be down to us to feel motivated to work hard so we can achieve the same or even more success than they are. We can do that only through the hard work and for that reason, we should be able to build our anti-procrastination mentality because we are eager to achieve success like the one that is being enjoyed by our peers as soon as possible.

In order to have that kind of motivating perspective during the comparison with our peers, we must believe that we have the ability to be the best from the hard work that we do and we must have that feeling of competitiveness inside of us. Believing that we can be the best among our peers will push us to prove that thought by working in our best capacity constantly in order to improve our current condition and the competitiveness personality will make us don't want to lose to anyone and put in the optimum effort in order to do that. When you have those two in your mindset in the work that you do, it makes you feel that you should not waste time to relax or enjoy some fun but unproductive activities because you want to demonstrate that faith in yourself is true to other people.

This is true also when it comes to building your motivation to work when you meet problems during the work process. Without a strong competitive feeling and the belief that you can be the best through the hard work that you do, you might feel even more discouraged if you do the comparison activity between your current condition and your peers' when you are in your low point. You see that people from your families or friends do well or even thriving with the work that they do. That can make you think of yourself as a failure, dent your confidence, and makes you lazy to do your work.

When it comes to this, you should remember that all people have their own problems in their work and they most probably already overcame some of theirs to get to the state where they are now. If you just stop working and procrastinating, then when are you going to be in the same or even in the further position than them in terms of success? Nothing good can come to you if you don't work for it. You must push yourself to overcome the problems that you currently have in work to have the chance to be in a similar position as your more successful peers. With that kind of perspective in mind, you should be able to build the continuation aspect in your anti-procrastination mentality so you can be more driven to get back up and keep going in your work despite the struggles that you have.

Do not feel discouraged when you see your peers succeed more as that kind of thinking can only be harmful to you. Instead, use it as a motivation for you to overcome the problems that you face, keep working, and avoid procrastination so you have the chance to beat that achievement of your peers in the future. That is the thing that need want to keep in mind so you can take advantage of the comparison activity that you do with your peers' condition.

Compare with Successful People

In the work that you do in your industry, there must be some people who already make it to the top. These people are special because of only a few that can achieve a big success in the work that they do. It takes a lot of consistent hard work so they can be in their position.

When you try to do a comparison with these successful people, you must have the belief that you can also accomplish the same or even more achievements that they do too. Only by having that kind of belief that you are able to work your way to realize it. After all, when you look at the success story of successful people who work their way up to their achievements, they usually start with a similar or even lower position from you in their work. Only by taking the time to put in the effort constantly that they are able to realize the goals that they have.

In that regard, you should also try to imitate what they have in terms of their resolve and their commitment to work so that you can build your anti-procrastination mentality in the way that they do too and are able to work with the same dedication as they have. Most successful people who work their way from the bottom must have an excellent work ethic that makes them able to avoid procrastination to work optimally.

This is also true too about the things that you can get from the comparison to face the problems that you may have at work. The road to success can be full of the things that prevent you to achieve success and successful people must have experienced some too in their work. By seeing that in the end those people can achieve the success that they have, it can add to your motivation to keep working so you can be in the same position as them eventually. This can in turn build up the continuation aspect also in your anti-procrastination mentality as you have a more resilient trait by learning from the approach that successful people have when they face the problems that they meet in their work.

When doing the comparison with successful people for your continuation aspect of anti-procrastination mentality, you can also do these things to further add your benefits:

- Learn from the similar problems that they have in their journey to success and what do they do in order to overcome these to achieve success. By understanding the approach that they use, it can probably be the solution that you need for the problems that you meet also in your work
- Read successful people autobiography to have more knowledge about how they work their way to success and what problems do they meet in their story. Sometimes when we look at successful people, we may only know about the results that they have achieved at the moment. By reading about their success story completely, we will know more about the struggles that they have already faced for our inspiration of continuity in the work that we do
- Get their sayings about failure and how it contributes to their success. Problems in work can often be seen as a failure for us. Successful people usually have their own sayings about how failures shape their way

to the success that they achieved. By reading them, we can get the motivation that we need to keep working on solving our problems and add to our perspective on how we should treat failures in our work

Successful people have their problems too that they have faced on the road to the top. by behaving in the same way that they do, which is to continue working to solve the problems and not procrastinate, we are able to achieve our success too in our work and build the continuation aspect in our mentality.

****

Comparison, as you can see, can benefit our motivation significantly to solve the problems that we meet in our work. Because only by the continuation of our work and not giving in to procrastination that we can get the results that we see from the ideal version of ourselves, our peers, or the successful people in the world.

Next, we will move on to the second pillar of the anti-procrastination mentality, which is the habit. Positive habits can enhance our anti-procrastination mentality significantly as we are able to get used to the things that benefit our work and make us less and less susceptible to procrastination while doing the habit. We will take a look at how some particular habits can shape the 3Cs of our anti-procrastination mentality, starting with the first C, Cause.

HABIT BUILD 1 – CAUSE: TRACK PROGRESS AND REFLECT

When we have the targets that we want to chase in our work and they have been noted by us as the things that we want to achieve as the result of our effort, then it can be good for us to have a habit of doing tracking process regularly to strengthen the benefits of the targets in our work and in the process of building our anti-procrastination mentality.

Targets, after all, can easily be forgotten once we have formulated them if we do not take a look at them regularly. By making it our habit to see what are the works that we have done and know whether the effort that we have put in has contributed to make us closer to our targets' realization, we can keep being reminded to the cause that we have for our work. That kind of habit can keep us working to the maximum by trying to make our progress faster to reach our goals.

Progress tracking activity can result in two kinds of results and each should be used as the push that we need to work hard. The first result is that we lag behind the things that we want to achieve in our work and it seems that we make slow progress. Knowing that, we should be more inspired to make our progress faster by working more diligently and effectively to try to catch up with the expectation. On the other hand, if we track our progress and find that we are in line with our expected progress or even exceed it, then we should be driven to keep our pace of work to ensure that the progress can be held or, even better, we try to work more so that we can make the progress to the realization of our targets even faster than what it already is.

In the activity of progress tracking, one thing that is important too is that we don't forget to do the reflection on what must we do so we can be better and improve ourselves in our work. There may be some points in the past when we still gave in to the urge of procrastination or we still have not worked as optimum as we should be. There can also be some approaches in our work that are not effective and can be updated so we can get the results that we want in a better way related to our targets. By using the result of our periodical reflection from the progress tracking that we do to our targets, then we can implement our thinking to work better in the future while also trying to be better in avoiding laziness in the effort to sharpen our anti-procrastination mentality. This is especially related to the strength of the cause that we want to achieve from our work.

The habit of progress tracking and evaluation of what we have done in our work can benefit us significantly when we want to utilize our cause to improve our chance of avoiding procrastination and keep on going with our work. In the following parts of the book, we will try to take a look at how this positive habit can be done more optimally to make us benefit even more.

Set Big Day Appraisal

Targets in our work usually take some time to be achieved, especially if they are the big ones that can be seen as some of the best achievements in our life if we finally realize them.

When we are in the pursuit to accomplish those big targets in our work, it is very easy to not paying attention to them gradually as the days go by. Ultimately, we can forget about them completely and our work can be distracted as a result of not having the objectives that it wants to pursue. The urge of procrastination can make itself more tempting to us as a result.

Because of this, we need to evaluate periodically for the targets that we want to achieve and the works that we have done. It is so that we can keep being reminded of the targets that we pursue in our work periodically too.

For the frequency to do the evaluation activity, it can be set according to our expectations of how long the targets that we have in our work should be completed. We can set a period of monthly, quarterly, or annually for the big progress tracking and reflection activity that we want to do in order to not losing the commitment that we have in our work as a result of having the targets.

By doing the progress tracking and reflection to our targets' pursuit in our work, it can have other benefits as well related to the anti-procrastination mentality that we try to build. We can constantly refine our approach to work and avoid procrastination in a comprehensive way by reflecting on the things that we have done during the period that we set as the one we do an evaluation on. We can also see our general thinking to the urge of procrastination that comes our way and understand if there is something that can be improved in our mindset in order to do better to chase our targets in the next period of work.

For example, when we have the target to have a certain amount of sales in the work that we do to our business, if we set a progress tracking and reflection period in every three months, then we can see how diligent the work that we have done in relation to our business in the past three months and whether that can result in the progress that we hope to achieve to get the sales targets. Is there probably some point during the period that we work lazily without strong reason for that kind of attitude which actually can probably be optimized to produce better results? What do we think when we give in to procrastination during the work hours in the three months period? Maybe we think that we can achieve what we want to by giving that kind of effort in our work while it turns out to be not true as we reflect on it in the period of three months? Is there anything that we should change in our mindset related to our work for the next three months so that things can be better? If you are a manager or a boss with some employees that work for you, then you can also do this evaluation periodically with them together in order to find out what you can do to be more optimal at work and avoid procrastination.

In doing progress tracking and reflection to the things that you have done in work and to the anti-procrastination mentality that you have built periodically, there are some things that may help you to optimize your time in work more and avoid procrastination:

- Try to allocate special hours to do the activity. By having a particular time just to do the periodical evaluation on your targets' achievement in relation to your work and anti-procrastination mentality, you should be able to get more thinking on it to improve your work and mentality in the next period

- Benchmark on the progress that the others have in the similar work of you have done in the period. You may have peers that do the work that can be seen as the same kind of work that you do. By doing comparison in your progress tracking and reflection activity on whether there are some things which they progress better than you, then you can improve your work and anti-procrastination mentality by taking a look at what they do in their work so they can progress better than you

- Be consistent in doing the periodical evaluation until your targets are achieved. The result of the activity can only barely be seen if you just do it once or twice as you cannot see the impact of the implementation for the things you think should be improved in the next evaluation. By doing the evaluation process constantly, you should be gradually better in finding a way to improve your work optimization and build your anti-procrastination mentality thus the improvement should be more noticeable to those

By doing the periodical appraisal of your progress and your optimization of time to work in the right way, you should be able to become more productive and avoid the activities that can have a bad effect on the progress from time to time.

Refine the Approach

As you do progress tracking and reflection on the work that you have done, you should be able to find the improvements that you can do to be better in terms of your work process and how you use your time to realize your targets. From there, you should refine your approach so you can be better at those processes in the future.

There is often a better way to optimize the work that you do and there can even be some methods or techniques that are found just recently that can be utilized to better serve your work optimization so you can use your work hours to produce more results. You should pay attention to things like that when you do an evaluation of your work so you can do more results after the activity.

When it comes to procrastination, there can be also a way that you can do to improve your approach to better handle it. There are some reasons that probably you find as the things that cause you the high urge to procrastinate in your work. For example, when you work in the past, there is a bottleneck from the activity that is done by your colleague which regularly makes you procrastinate as you should wait for the colleague to finish his/her job before you can get on with yours. By noticing this in your evaluation activity, you can act to fix it by probably discuss with your colleague how the bottleneck can be solved so you have fewer reasons to procrastinate with your work or you can anticipate it by doing the things that can be done in parallel while waiting for the work results from your colleague. Things like that may not be noticed if you just get on with your work every day and don't put the time to do some progress tracking and reflection activity.

As you refine your approach so you can be more optimal in the time that you need to work, remember to always relate it to the targets that you want to achieve in your work. Some approaches might be better when it comes to particular targets but they might be less effective when you use them to chase another set of targets. For example, if your target in your work for the production division of the company is to successfully meet the production target for a particular product, then probably you should focus your approach in trying to improve the reliability rate of production machines that are related to the production of that product to prevent them to breakdown when they produce the product rather than doing the improvement for all of the company production machines. That all machines approach may lessen your focus from something that is more important to the success of your target and can cause a bottleneck in the production process for that particular product. That, in turn, can cause procrastination in your work that actually can be prevented by focusing in improving the production machines that are directly related to the production process of the product instead.

Doing the approach refinement can be something that can boost your progress to the things that you want to realize. You should spare time to do it during your progress tracking and reflection activity to make your work optimization better in the working hours that you have in the future.

Take Time to Evaluate Daily

Besides the periodic evaluation that has been discussed earlier, it will be great if you can spare a little time at the end of every work day to do a daily evaluation of the progress of your targets. That way, you can implement continuous improvement in your quest to optimize time for work and sharpen the anti-procrastination mentality that you have in relation to the targets that you set. Besides, you can keep getting reminded of your cause as the additional motivation that you may need to keep on working hard.

When you do a daily evaluation of your work, you will remember more small details than you have in periodic evaluation, which takes a more general, big picture approach in your work and your effort to build an anti-procrastination mentality. Doing the daily progress tracking and reflection to the targets that you have and the work that you have done makes you notice the small details that may play a big part in the procrastination that you have done in your work hours. Thus, you can repair that immediately and will be able to get the improvement result faster too.

For an example, when you work today, you might realize in your daily evaluation that you give in to procrastination when you talk to your friends for a long time and as a result, that reduce the time that you can use for your work. By noticing this, you may want to limit the time that you do for talking with your colleagues and reserve it for some other time when you have done your work. That way, you should have more time to complete your work while having the time to talk to after you have done it.

Those kinds of little things that will be noticed by daily evaluation can be the improvement that you need to keep being committed to the cause of your work.

When you try to do a daily evaluation for your work in relation to your targets, there are some things that you may find useful to remember:

- Try to have some to-do list to base your daily evaluation from. When you begin your day, you can write some of the things that you want to do today in relation to your targets. Base your daily evaluation at the end of the day on that to see what are the things that can be done to improve your rate of completing them while also thinking about the work that should be done in the next day
- Note the important details during your day in work that you think you should pay attention to in your daily evaluation but you may forget them. There are some little details which can be important but can be forgotten if you do not note them. By doing the note taking, you can think more thoroughly about what is the best thing that you can do in regards to that part of the work that you note when you do the daily evaluation later
- Have a fixed time to do it at the end of the day. By allocating around 15 minutes at the end of your day to do the daily evaluation, you should have enough time to reflect on what has been going through in your work day, your daily progress to targets, and what you can do tomorrow so you can be better in terms of optimizing your work and avoiding procrastination

When you have made daily evaluation activity as a habit of yours, then you can improve step-by-step in terms of optimizing the time that you have for working and chasing your targets.

****

Thus, you have learned more about how the habit of progress tracking and reflection on your work can help you in building a strong anti-procrastination mentality especially related to the cause aspect that you have in work. Next, we will see another habit that you can utilize to significantly shape your anti-procrastination mentality that is related to scheduling.

HABIT BUILD 2 – CONSISTENCY: FORMULATE WORK SCHEDULE

In terms of positive habits, formulating work schedules that you can implement every day can be the thing that you need to maintain your consistency in work and sharpen your anti-procrastination mentality.

When you have a schedule to guide the time that you have in a day, then you should be able to avoid procrastination more because you know exactly when you need to work and when you need to relax after you have done your work. This can make the consistency that you need in terms of working can be easier to achieve.

When you have formulated the work schedule for yourself, then you should have a high eagerness to maintain it. When the time in the day is for you to do your work, you should stay as far away as possible to the things that can distract you and can give you the urge to procrastinate as your resolve to maintain it. Try to be disciplined so that you can optimize your time for work to get the best results that you want from it.

That discipline to work can only be gained by implementing it day by day. For better results, the work schedule that you have built should be adapted to the time that you have available for your work on that day. The time that you have for your work every day may be different as you have different things that you need to spare your time daily. When you try to build the discipline to implement your work schedule, try to be sensitive too about the realistic time that you have for work when formulating it. That way it can be easier for you to follow through on the schedule that you have created.

The workload that you have is also something that should be considered too in formulating your work schedule. When you have much workload that you need to do on that day, then you should try to adjust your working hours to be able to do it optimally. Try to allocate enough work time for you so it can be completed on time on that day. It may need to consume of the time that you have allocated to relax after your work but if it must be done then you should find some time to do the work. To avoid having to do this kind of thing, try to adjust your schedule to work on the future task that you may need to complete when you have the time on some days before. That may be the thing that you need to do so you are not burdened with too much work that you have to finish in a tight deadline. A work that is completed with time pressure can produce a rash and careless work result which is not good for everyone involved.

If you can be committed in terms of formulating and doing the work schedule, then the impact on your work consistency should be positive. You can become a more organized person in your work during the day and you have known the approximate time that you need to do your workload so you are more motivated to finish it during the time span given and avoid the urge that you have to relax in that time. That can build up the consistency that you need for your anti-procrastination mentality and you should be able to consistently optimize the time that you have for work once you get used to this.

When you try to implement this work schedule habit for your anti-procrastination mentality in the work consistency aspect, there are some things that you can do in the implementation. You should try to clearly establish the division between work hours and relaxing hours, be able to formulate a detailed work schedule to guide you weekly and daily, and also build the discipline that you need to implement the work schedule well. All of them will be discussed in more detail below.

Divide the Work and Relaxation Hours

When you build work schedule and you want a noticeable effect for your anti-procrastination mentality in terms of your consistency in work, you should try to divine first the hours that you can have for two big activities of your day: work and relaxation activities.

Doing this will help to establish a clear division in your mind between the time that you need to work and the time when you can relax. Hence, when you are in the work hours that you have defined for yourselves, you should be able to concentrate more on working and do not pay attention to the urge of procrastination that you may have. It is because that you have known that there will be time to do relaxation and other fun activities that are not related to work. You can work with more concentration as a result of that.

This division of working and relaxation hours can be different day by day. There are probably some days which are more special than the others when you need to work more as a result of a tight deadline in your work or if there is something that you need to do faster for a significantly better result. There can also be some days when you need to not working as much as usual as there are family matters that you must attend to or there are important things that you need to do with your friends. However, in the other ordinary days, you may have a fixed schedule on working and relaxing hours. It is important to be flexible when you need to in the division of working and relaxation hours but you should be able to maintain your standard working and relaxation hours in most days.

There are some considerations that you may need to think of when establishing the line for the time in a day for these two activities:

- Work on further tasks beforehand if your standard working hours in the day allows you to. If you have more time as a result of a small number of works that need to be done at the day, then it might be good for you to allocate similar work hours as your ordinary day and not add the relaxation hours. Try to work on other tasks that have a longer deadline as you may do not have the time to do it properly when it is already near of its deadline

- Do not be too generous in giving relaxation hours to yourself in a day. Too much relaxation hours that you schedule in a day may result in planned procrastination altogether. Remember your work targets and try to achieve it as soon as possible by allocating the needed work hours to do that. Eight to ten hours should be the minimum standard that you have in working hours on a workday

- Be strict if the condition allows when you implement your schedule. Your work hours may need to be extended from the original plan that you may already formulate as a result of a sudden work that you need to do or your relaxation hours might need a longer time as there is a sudden family needs that you should take care of. Be flexible in those special circumstances but try to maintain it if there are nothing extraordinary

- Adjust the division to your preferred work time if possible. You have understood about a preferred work time that you may have in work from the previous chapter of the book. If possible, try to include that thought into your division of work and relaxation hours by including the period when you feel you have the best mood for work in your working hours and allocate your relaxation hours in other periods of the day

- Divide it by accommodating other people that work with you too. On some days, you might need to meet and interact with other people who are related to the work that you do. Try to think about that when you set up this general division of activities period

This working and relaxation hours division are meant to be the general guidelines that you need to have so you can establish consistency in the working hours when you need to think about doing your job and not giving in to the urge of procrastination. That relaxation can be done at some other time when you have allocated hours for it.

After the general guidance, you have to detail it further to give you clarity in terms of what you will do in the working hours. This will be discussed next.

Determine Weekly and Daily Details

After you have set the general division of working and relaxation hours, it is time to dive into the details of your working hours. The question that you will ask is: what do I have to do in these working hours that I have allocated to optimize my work?

When you try to define the details in your working hours, you need to think about what are the activities that can be done and what are the results that you need to achieve on that day. You may have your to-do list for the activities that you plan to do in that day. However, you need to find the balance between your to-do lists and the schedule that you have in terms of the working hours available to you. Put those activities that are listed in your to-do list based on its prioritization and how much hours that should be allocated to each of the activity in your work schedule. Something that is more urgent and prioritized to be done should be placed earlier if possible so you can have the most important works done first before you have to attend other works. This is so that you will not think of those urgent tasks that can distract your mind when you do other things.

If you try to formulate the details of your work schedule, then you should know about the restriction that you may have in the day about your work hours. Some days may need this extra number of working hours and some other days may only allow you to work for this limited number. Because of that reason too, we restrict ourselves to manage the details of your work schedule on a weekly and daily basis, not further in the future. It is so you have more knowledge in detail of the number of working hours that you have in the days in which you plan your detailed activities.

By the order of the formulation, when you are in the weekend or early in the weekday, you should try to formulate your weekly schedule from the working hours that you have in the week. This must be aligned with the results that you expect to be had in that week and you should also think about the tasks that can still be worked in later weeks but it can also be worked to in the week that you plan your schedule currently. When you plan your work schedule before you start your week, you may just now the estimation of the working hours that you have in the later workdays of it. That is okay because you will fix your schedule in the daily details before you begin that day. However, this weekly schedule is important to formulate to give you a big picture of what things that you can expect to work on in that week so you can optimize your time better.

After you define your weekly schedule in the available work hours that you have, then try to check on it again when you arrive on the day before or early in the day when you should run the schedule. You check whether the tasks planned before is still relevant then adapt it to your needs. That way you can set your daily schedule sharper from the tasks that you have planned according to your weekly target. It can become more detailed and accustomed to the new requirement that you may just find before you work in the day.

When planning your weekly and daily schedule, try to be detail in your planned activities in terms of the time that you set on them. Having the schedule as detailed as 15 minutes period can be ideal and give you some feeling of certainty for the guidance that the schedule will have for your day. That effect can give you more power in terms of your work consistency in the anti-procrastination mentality that you try to build for the work that you do.

From the explanation that has been given, here is a quick summary of the things that you need to pay attention to when formulating your weekly and daily schedule:

- Ask yourself what you can do to optimize your time in the working hours using your planned activities in the schedules
- Base them on your to-do list and have the activities with the most urgency and priority to be worked on first
- Consider the restriction that you may have in the day's working hours. Some days may have more or less working hours available than the standard working day of yours
- Formulate weekly schedule first based on your approximate weekly targets from the big goals that you have. Then, sharpen it to daily schedule before or early in the related day according to the new details or restrictions that may apply

- Be as detail as 15 minutes time frame for your schedules if you can

By having your weekly and daily schedule ready to guide your working hours, you should be more prepared to optimize your time and avoid procrastination in terms of the consistency in your work. However, all that planning will be in vain without the discipline to implement them. How can you improve your discipline to run the schedule so it can make your work process better and more productive?

Implement with Discipline

When it comes to make sure you get the result that you want, you should always balance excellent planning with excellent execution. That is also true for the planning of the work schedule that you have made. You should be able to implement it well so you can get the optimum impact from your work schedule for your work consistency.

How that can be done? By enforcing the discipline that you have in its execution.

The urge of procrastination can come during your working hours despite the planning that you have made to it. If you give in to that feeling in your head, then you will abandon the work plan that you have made and just stop working to enjoy your time with some other activities. That cannot be good for your anti-procrastination mentality as that can build up into a bad lazy habit in your work.

Thus, you should try to have discipline in implementing the working schedule that you have put in the effort to formulate. There are some things that you can do to improve your discipline in implementing it:

- Note and have the daily work schedule that you have made close to you. That way you can always access it when you need to take a look at what you should do in a particular timeframe of the day

- When you have the urge to procrastinate, remember the relaxing hours that you have planned for yourselves aside from the working hours. That way you can hold the thought of relaxing and do other activities outside work to that period

- Arrange some rewards and punishments that you can have depending on whether you succeed or fail in holding the urge to procrastinate during your working hours. This can be done especially in the early stage of your work schedule tools implementation when you probably still do not have enough discipline to implement it without some extra drive. For the example of rewards and punishment, you can treat yourself a coffee at the end of your working hours if you succeed to go through it without procrastinating but you need to cut your relaxing hours tomorrow if you fail to work optimally on that day. That should make you more motivated to stay discipline on your working hours

- Tell other people about your working hours. By doing this, they will not try to bother you with unimportant things during your work schedule while you also feel more accountable as other people can see whether you work or not in the period that you have told them

- Use reminder tools for the details of the activities that you must do in your working hours. Simple tools like alarm in your phone or activities prompt software on your laptop can be just the things that you need to maintain the tracking of your planned work schedule. Set it before you begin your working hours in the day for all of the days' planned activities

Your work schedule can be the best schedule that a human has ever made but without enough resolve to do the activities planned in it, then it will be just something formulated in vain without a result. The points above can help you in making sure you stay disciplined in executing your work schedule.

****

As you have seen, the work schedule formulation can be an important thing to have if you do it right. Consistency in your work can be had and you can also build the barrier for procrastination in the time when you should work in that day by using the work schedule tool.

In the next chapter, we will see about the habit that can help you build a continuation in your anti-procrastination mentality. This is a kind of mentality that you build in yourself to be resistant to the failures and struggles that you may meet in your work process. We will discuss what can you do to build that kind of mentality to support your anti-procrastination campaign next.

HABIT BUILD 3 – CONTINUATION: SHAPE THE BULLET PROOF MENTALITY

During the work that you do constantly, there can be some points when you fail or meet some frustration in the process because there are problems that you seem to not be able to solve. At that time, the urge for procrastination can come much stronger because you are more stressed at work than you usually are and you have more desire to relax or do other things as long as it does not make you face the stress that you have in your work.

Well, that is surely one of the things that will test your anti-procrastination mentality strongly as it is sometimes hard to escape from that desire to procrastinate during the time when you seem stuck with your work. It can be hard especially if it counts as one of your first times that you meet problems in your work. Only through the habit that you try to build in getting back up again to try to solve the problems that you meet and overcome the failures that you experience in work that you can be more resistant to the desire of procrastination in this testing time. The desire to delay or abandon the work that you do in your working hours when you feel stress as a result of the bad experiences in it can be hard to prevent indeed unless you already have a strong habit for it.

There can be a number of times when you meet the frustration of failures at work. As you overcome the frustration each time you meet it and limit your procrastination along the way to keep working, you can keep building the momentum for the continuation aspect in your anti-procrastination mentality to grow stronger. As you make a habit out of it and keep on working hard despite the setbacks that you have, you should be able to shape the bulletproof mentality that you need so you can be strong and overcome all of the struggles that you have to achieve success in your work.

That way, you should be able to make success easier to come to you as a result of your consistent hard work and have a strong chance to not procrastinate despite the failures that you have to face in work. After all, nothing can stop you from doing the work that you want to do and you continue to work to make your situation better than the failure that you have experienced.

Remember also that when you give in to the procrastination when you face setbacks, it will be harder for you to come back and you can make yourself go deeper in the desire to not work. That can happen because you do not think that you can solve the bad situation by the work that you do and as a result, you will not try to work your way out, becoming lazier and lazier because of that. You should try your best to avoid that kind of bad cycle and put in the best effort to get out of the situation as soon as possible. Just think that only you can change the situation that you are currently in by doing the hard work.

It is your choice to shape your mentality to the one that can take failure as a sign to keep on working, probably even harder, to overcome the bad thing that you face or to the one that keeps procrastinating more and more when it meets the struggles and challenges that it must solve to move forward.

If you choose to shape a bulletproof mentality to support your anti-procrastination intention, then you can try some of the following tips to help you to do that: try to fail as early as possible, think and execute the way to get out of the situation as fast as you can, and, on the more testing situation when you must, give yourself some time to calm down but place the fixed time for you to come back to work. All of these things will be discussed in more detail next.

Fail Early, Succeed Early

Now, this is not to say that you should let yourself intentionally falling to failure when you work. As being said earlier, you should try to avoid failure as best as possible.

This suggestion asks you instead to work as fast and as good as you can so you can face the struggles and problems that you need to face and overcome them quickly too. That way, you should be able to succeed early as a result of the experiences and lessons that you have gathered on your work in a quick fashion.

When you want to fail early and succeed early, the thing that you have to emphasize on yourself is this question: have you optimized the time that you have got for work and not leaving a room to procrastinate during that? By ensuring that you have already worked optimally to utilize all of the working hours that you have, you should be able to navigate your way in the road to success quicker than anyone else.

By failing early, you also have the chance to build a strong continuation aspect in the anti-procrastination mentality soon too. That way, you are able to be resistant to the urge of procrastination in the face of adversity faster too because you have built the experience that can help you to be surer of your commitment to work even during the bad situation of your work.

Failing early in a positive way like that is not easy though as there can be many things that prevent you to work as quickly as you can. Here are some tips to help you with that and build a strong anti-procrastination mentality that you want to have by doing so:

- Aim to test the work result that you have earlier before you have the obligation to officially submit it. By trying to test it beforehand, you should be able to detect and repair some failures in it, if any, early and make you faster in work by trying to have it finished well before the due date to have it tested first.

- Spare some time to think about the most effective way to do your work. As we often do our works without thinking about the plan to do them better beforehand, we can miss some ways that can actually make our work results produced much earlier. By allocating some small window in our days for it, we can uncover the possibilities and make them work for us

- Keep updating yourself with the latest approach to work. As time goes by, there can be new methods discovered that can be tried in the work of yours and they have the potential to save your time. Update yourself regularly regarding that to see the possibilities and implement the ones that you find to try the effect for your work

- Delegate tasks if possible or look at some help for the work that you need. There can be times when you cannot do your work effectively without some support from others. Delegate the works that you have when appropriate or ask other people about the way your work should be done. Asking other people can make you know about how to do your work better and faster. Eventually, you can allocate the time that you have saved to finish other things related to your work

- Work on other things when you have finished the works that you intend to do that day. Your daily targets may have already been finished and there is some time left before the end of your working hours. You should utilize it for working at other things instead of procrastinating so you can make them finished earlier too

By implementing the ways that can help you finish your work faster and not spending your working hours on the things that are unproductive, you should be able to fail earlier and succeed earlier. Just remember that when you meet the problems at work, you should embrace them and try to see them as the moments when you can learn and improve yourself in the work that you do. Most importantly, of course, you should try to solve the problems as soon as you can so you are able to move forward past them.

Formulate and Implement the Way Out Soon

When you meet with failures on your work process, there can be a desire to take some time away from it during your working hours and delay the work that you need to do to solve your situation. You should not do that if possible, though, because the longer that you take to start working on things to solve your problems, the harder it can get for you to trigger the motivation that you need to start working on it. You should try to think and implement the way out of the failure situation as soon as possible so you can have the discipline to continue working without any delay even when you meet some struggles along the way.

That kind of work continuity is important to be maintained in the midst of failure. After all, if you delay your work, then the urge to procrastinate can be harder and harder to ignore. As a result, you go to relax and do some other things which are not related to work during your working hours. You waste your time when it can be used to work on the solution that you need to get back up from the failures that you have experienced at work. That can weaken the resolve that you need to build a strong anti-procrastination mentality that you want to have.

The main thing here is that you should not weaken your drive to work even in the midst of adversity like failure. If ever, this should be the time when you should work harder instead of procrastinating so you can solve the problems immediately on the top of the regular works that you need to do every day. The first step that you take towards righting the failure immediately after it occurs can be the thing that you need to keep the constant of your work instead of you procrastinate immediately after it.

In terms of trying to come back soon from the failure that you have had in your work, it can be sometimes hard to do. Here are some tips for you to be able to do that:

- Benchmark for the solution. The problem that you have can be already faced by some other people. Try to see what is the best practice of coming back from the failure so you can do that also in your work
- List of all the possible solutions that you can think of and implement the one that seems to be more promising before you try the others if it does not work. There can multiple possible solutions for the failure in your work. Think of the possible alternatives and do the one that seems better for you before trialing others so you can get back up from the situation quicker
- Relate to the similar kinds of failures that you have faced before. There can be some other times in the past when you have found yourselves facing the struggles that you are able to overcome. The solution for your current problem probably more or less similar to the bad situation that you found yourself in before

- Make it your short-term work targets to solve the problems that you have. The targets can make you more disciplined in trying to overcome the situation in your work. Try to be committed to solve them in your work and accomplish the targets that you have set

- Get to the root cause of your failure. The real reason for your failure may not be the one that is seen on the surface. Try to see the root cause by asking why a few times on the things that are shown up to deal with the situation more effectively

Get back up from the failure that you find yourself in as soon as possible is important for the continuation of your work while avoiding the procrastination urge that may come as you spend more time in the dwelling on the struggles that you have to face. Implementing the tips given above might be the things that you need to do for that.

Place the Time to Get Back
It will be best if you can directly work to fix things as soon as the failure happens so you don't get a chance to procrastinate and waste your working hours. But what if the situation is unique that it is best for you to stay away from your work for a while? For example, the failure that happens to you in your business affects your relationship with your family so you need to attend to that thing first before you can put full concentration on your work. Or the failure that you do in your work at the office makes you lose your job in the company so you need some time to think about what you want to do next. What should you do in times like this so you don't fall to the procrastination trap?

Well, if you need some time to stay away from your work because it is unavoidable, then you should do it as it will be better for you if you handle other things first before going back to work and put in the effort again to come back from your failure. But you should put in the limit on when you want to come back after reflecting how long is the time that you need to stay away from your work and do other things. That way you can stay discipline to continue your work while also put the deadline for yourself to handle those other things besides work as you need it.

How long you should put the time to get back to your work? Well, you should think of the time which you can get back to your work as soon as possible so you can fix and overturn the situation at your job immediately but also the length of time that you need to be able to give enough period for you to attend the other problems besides your work. In other words, you should set the ideal time for you to get back to work which is not too soon but not too long for your other problem's solution. After all, it will not be good for your work if you keep on thinking on other matters if you have not finished them yet. However, you should be committed to that timeline that you make so you don't delay your come back to work. Don't let procrastination pulls you from coming back to your work because you keep delaying.

Here are some tips that can be useful for you if you need to delay your come back to work:

- If you have finished your other matters before the time that you have set, then it might be better for you to come back for work faster than the timeline plan so you can turn the situation in your work faster
- Completely switch your focus to the things other than work if possible. By being able to do that, you could accomplish the task quicker. Do not pay attention to the things related to work if possible until the time that you decide to go back to your work
- Allocate the hours that are usually reserved for your working hours to attend that other matters. By doing

this, you should be able to give enough time for them to be resolved in time with the plan that you have made

The most important point here is to set a deadline for you to attend the other matters and come back to your work as soon as possible. This is done so that you don't divide your attention with other matters when you want to focus to turn things around for your work, you don't build procrastination habit while away from work, and you ensure that the continuity in your work for building your anti-procrastination mentality can be maintained.

****

By shaping your bulletproof mentality after each failure that you meet in your work, you should be able to avoid procrastination that usually comes stronger with it by maintaining or even improving your work rhythm to overturn the condition and lead yourself on the way to success.

Next, we will move to the last pillar of the anti-procrastination mentality, which is focus. Focus is important to keep your attention to your work and not to the other things unrelated to it during your working hours. The first thing we will discuss is how to bring focus to improve your cause in a strong anti-procrastination mentality.

FOCUS BUILD 1 – CAUSE: SHARPEN YOUR GOALS

Goals can be different from each of us especially when it is related to the work that you do. After all, the nature of our work and the details of what we do in it can be distinct and so that brings some effect to the goals that we have. But, although different, one of the most important things to make sure about is that you need to get your goals narrow and sharp whatever your goals are.

The reason? Because by doing that, you will bring more focus to the things that you want to achieve at work. Imagine if you have 50 goals instead of 5 goals. What do you think will happen in your work because of that? When you have 50 goals, you will be confused because you have so many targets that you don't know what you should do precisely in your work to realize them. By only having 5 goals, you should be able to work more on the details that you need to focus according to your goals and this should result in a higher chance for you to accomplish the goals.

Your goals sharpness can also be seen in the scope that each of your goals has. Sharper goals should not have a very large scope as that can also help you in the focus of your work. The simple example is if you have the goal of becoming the vice president in your office, then it might be better for you to narrow the scope to the vice president of marketing. That should make you know more what are the things that you should do to realize your goals than if you target the goals with a very wide scope.

Besides having an effect in terms of the realization chance of your goals, the level of your goals' focus can also impact your anti-procrastination mentality, especially related to the cause aspect in the 3Cs that define your barrier to the urge of procrastination. If you have too many goals that are very wide in their scope, then there will be a higher chance for you to procrastinate in your work. It is because you might have less clue in what you should do to achieve your targets and you will have an abstract and fuzzy picture of the goals that you should pursue as one of the main motivations in your work. This should result in much lower drive to achieve the things that you want at work. Less drive means the bigger chance for you to be lazy and not focus on the work that you do.

Therefore, sharpening your goals is an important activity for you to build a strong anti-procrastination mentality and focus on the work that you do. Thus, you better know what things that you can do in order to make this cause aspect in your work becomes a thing that will help you to be more optimal in your job.

To do that, I suggest three things that can do that to you: list all the goals that you want to achieve before narrowing them down into a couple of the most important goals for you, set up the targets that have a top-down approach to it, and consider the time that you have and need to allocate to accomplish each of the goals. For a clearer understanding, we will discuss the three of them deeper in the next parts.

Think Big, Pick Small

You have so many things that you want to accomplish by doing your work. That is understandable. All of us also want to get many things in life and it will be very great if they are all attained. However, for the sharper focus of your work, you should try to narrow them down to a few.

This is important because, as humans, we can only put our attention to a small number of things at the same time. The research by the University of Oregon professors says that most of us can only focus on 4 things at most in time.

Therefore, we should try to limit our focus to our targets by keeping it around that number to make it more optimized for the focus of our work and anti-procrastination mentality. That is the way also that we can make sure all of them can have enough attention from us during our work and we do not procrastinate as a result of getting bogged down with too many things that we need to accomplish.

When you try to think what are the few goals that you should focus on, you can begin by listing all of the goals that you currently have in mind. It is better if you can note them down in a piece of paper. After that, you can pick the few (probably 3-5 targets) that seem are the most important and meaningful targets for you in your work. Choose them from the many goals that you have. That way, you can be sure that you do not miss any goals that might be important but you have not thought about related to your work and you make sure that you have already considered all the goals that you want to have before settling on a few of them. This is the way that you can think big and pick small for the targets that you have at work.

There are also some other things that you can consider to do while selecting your targets:

- Make sure that the targets that you pick can directly result from the work that you do. That way, you do not have to spread your focus to do other things that can distract your work
- Combine some targets that you have from the list if necessary. There can be some targets that you have from the so many things that you want to achieve which can actually be merged to produce a stronger target that can represent its combined elements. If

you see them, then do the combination to make the result one of the stronger things that you want to target

- Evaluate the few targets that you have picked to sharpen them further. There can be some further enhancement that you can do in the targets that you have chosen from the big list. Reflect on them to see if there is anything that you should do to make them serve as much better motivation for your work
- Imagine what will you feel and the effect when you achieve each of the targets in the list. The importance and meaning of the targets for you can be assessed by the thinking what you have and feel when you imagine your accomplishment of them. Give higher priority for the targets that can make you happy and proud while having the biggest positive impact for you and the people around you
- Discuss with other people to select the targets if you need to. People close to you or your mentor can give valuable suggestions and feedback related to the targets that you want to focus on. Have a conversation with them about your targets to get them

After you have picked the few targets which you think are the most important for you to focus on your work, you can think about what are the stepping stones that you need to walk into in order to eventually achieve the things that you want in your work. This can be important to further sharpen your goals so you can optimize your work and strengthen the cause aspect in your anti-procrastination mentality more. We will discuss more about this in the next part.

Set Up Gradual Targets
When you try to set targets for your work, often you end up having big achievements in life that you want to accomplish.

That is completely fine and that can be a big source of motivation for you to work and avoid procrastination.

However, having big targets can have its downside also in terms of the difficulty that you may see as it can be very hard for you to *directly* reach the goals and how you are very far in your current work when you see where you want to be. To mitigate this, we should set up gradual targets from the big targets that we have to make it seems easier and more step-by-step to reach them.

By setting up gradual targets in your work, you can make the targets sharper in each phase down to the smallest milestones that you make. And more reachable too. That can bring a good boost to your motivation in working on them. You can also be more focused at work with the sharper goals in mind knowing also that by achieving them, then you can be a step closer to reach the original targets that you initially hope to achieve.

When you set gradual targets from the original goals that you have in your work, you should set deadlines too for them and that depends on the deadline that you have set yourself to the original big goals. If, for example, you expect the original goals in your work to be accomplished five years from now, then you should set the gradual targets' deadline shorter than that e.g. in a year, three months, and a month. The gradual targets, of course, should represent a downgrade in each lower phase of the deadline but it should always be correlated with the original targets that you intend to achieve. Hence, the gradual targets that you set will support the eventual accomplishment of the original targets.

Besides that thing that you should note when you want to do this, here are some other suggestions for you to set gradual goals that can help to sharpen your goals and build the cause aspect for your anti-procrastination mentality:

- Make the gradual targets' deadline in line with the big day appraisals period that has been discussed earlier in the habit build. That way you can keep track and evaluate the progress of your eventual cause achievement with the insight of the realization for your gradual targets

- Set gradual targets that can be measured quantitatively. This is related to the function of them as sharper goals that support your intention to achieve original targets. By having them can be tracked in numbers, you can be sure that they are sharper and you will know better about what you need to focus on your work to reach them

- Formulate gradual targets that can motivate you to work hard while can be realistically achieved. Set them in an optimistic way while remembering that they should be able to be accomplished with your work. Balance is the key here to make you get the right motivation from the attraction of your gradual targets

- Benchmark the progress of the successful people whose current state can be likened to your original goals for the materials of your gradual targets. By doing that, you can be sure that you have a role model that you can follow the path of in your work while setting the gradual targets that can motivate you to be as successful as them

- Set a deadline in terms of setting the gradual targets. As time goes by and as you work deeper in your job, you might want to change the gradual targets that you have to the less challenging ones. By having a deadline for that, you can be sure that you still have the targets that are in line and support you to eventually reach your original goals. The deadline for each of the phases for your gradual targets do not have to be the same, though (e.g. You set the deadline of your three months targets a day before you begin the period and you set the deadline of your annual targets a day before you begin that annual period too, not a day before your three months period)

For an example of the gradual targets set for the original targets that you have in your work are:

- Original Target (5 years from now): Become the VP in the Production area of my company
- Gradual Target 1 (3 years from now): Become the Assistant VP in the Production area of my company
- Gradual Target 2 (1 year from now): Become the Senior Manager in the Production area of my company
- Gradual Target 3 (6 months from now): Achieve 90% monthly production target
- Gradual Target 4 (3 months from now): Achieve 85% monthly production target
- Gradual Target 5 (1 month from now): Achieve 80% monthly production target

That is a simple illustration of the gradual targets. The ones that you use are, of course, solely up to you and should be tailored to your original targets. The important thing to remember is that you should make them sharp goals that make you feel motivated to achieve them as stepping stones to reach your final targets. That way, they should help you in working optimally and build the cause aspect for a strong anti-procrastination mentality.

Consider the Time

One of the important characteristics that a sharp goal should have is that it is realistic in relation to the time that you need to accomplish it. Unrealistic goals that you put in a very tight deadline can affect you in the laziness to work as you do not think that you can achieve the targets that you have set however hard you work.

This does not mean that you cannot set yourself very big targets in the work that you do. That, of course, can be done and the bigger the goal is then the more you should feel motivated to accomplish it. But to do that, you should consider the time that you put in the plan to achieve them. Bigger goals probably require you to set a longer period to put in your effort so you can achieve them in the planned timeframe that you have.

Time is something that is important to consider in setting the goals because it is a finite resource to each of us. No person can have more time in a day than the others. So, you must include time in your thinking to know what kinds of targets that you should set in a period. If you take a time approach first when you consider your targets and you have to set targets in two years' time, then consider what are the accomplishments that can be done at that time. You have to think also about your current condition and how far it is to get to the destinations that you desire.

By considering the time that you need to achieve your goals, you should be able to sharpen your goals even further and optimize your working hours more as a result.

When considering the time factor for your targets, there are some things that you can do to ensure the results of that are better:

- Project the work that you need to do to make your targets a reality. How does the workload look and how long that you should allocate so it can be done? By doing that, you should have a more realistic prediction of the time to reach your targets

- See the history of the duration that your targets need to have in order for them to be realized. There might be people who have achieved the things that you want in your work before. Compare the time that you have set for your targets with the ones that are done by the other people to get a big picture in how you should set the targets that you want related to time
- Consider the standard working hours that you have in a day in regards to achieving the targets. The working hours that you have in a period can see whether time can be a problem in achieving the targets that you have set. Think about this factor too when you set your targets

By setting the targets that already have time factor considered in them, they should be sharper to guide you in your work and support you significantly in avoiding procrastination that you can have in the working hours.

****

Setting sharp goals with the suggested focus methods described above can empower the cause aspect in your anti-procrastination mentality so you can work more diligently as a result of having motivating, impactful, yet achievable goals in your work.

Next up, we will discuss the focus implementation in terms of your work consistency. In this, we will try to remove the significant distractions that you can have in work to make you much more focused and can accomplish more results in the working hours that you have.

FOCUS BUILD 2 – CONSISTENCY: MOVE AWAY FROM DISTRACTIONS

Think about the time when you worked previously. There can be some things that distract you a moment or two from your work before you can go back and do your job again. If it only takes few minutes from your working hours seldomly, then it can probably be still counted as okay as it is very rare for you to be able to utilize your working hours 100% optimal. However, it can become a problem if the distractions take a proportionate amount of time in your working hours or if they distract you only for a short time but they happen quite often so you cannot focus on your work completely.

The examples of the distractions that usually can take away significant amount of our working hours are social media and conversation about non-job things with co-workers. Tell the truth, how much time do you actually spend browsing the feed of your social media during the time that you work? How long is the time that you use to discuss the latest office gossips with your co-workers? I imagine the proportion will be much if we add them up and compare the result to the total working hours that you have.

In fact, there has already been research about this that proves distractions can take a major part of our working hours. According to the Bureau of Labor Statistics study, the average worker spends less than three hours of working hours to do the job that he/she should do (in the amount of 2 hours and 53 minutes to be exact) as a significant time is being spent on distractions that they have in work. That means that most of us truly work less than 50% of the standard working hours in a day (8 hours). That also shows, somehow ironically, how much potential that can be had if you can optimize the working hours that you have and moving away from the distractions that you have at work. By doing that, you should be able to be more productive in terms of time more than two times of the average worker!

Now, trying to focus completely on work and not paying attention to the distractions that we have around us is, of course, not going to be easy. There is a reason why the urge of procrastination from those distractions can win most of the workers' time as we have seen in the data presented to us. They can be so tempting, especially when we are currently stressed with the work that we do and want to have a break from it. When you are frustrated with the work that you have and your co-workers seem to have a fun discussion near you, then who should we blame if we abandon the work that we do and approach our guys to know what is the fun that they talk about? When there is a notification of a recent post in your social media from a close friend of yours, what can we do other than open our smartphone to see and give our response to it? Those reactions to the distractions that come in our work can actually result in a long time to procrastinate as we move on further to discuss other fun things with our co-workers or scroll our social media feed longer to see other posts that might interest us. As a result, our work is abandoned and delayed for a longer time than it should be.

So, what can we do to anticipate those distractions and be strong enough to avoid most of them so your work can be done more productively in the working hours that you have? Well, I have some suggestions that you can do: list the things that give significant contribution to the unproductive portion of your working hours, clear up your thoughts to focus on work, and set up the necessary prevention for the distractions that you have in your work. We will take a look deeper into each of these suggestions below to help you in utilizing them to optimize your work and support the build of the consistency aspect in your anti-procrastination mentality.

Define the Things That Disturb You
If you have the knowledge of the distractions that you think are the hardest to avoid during your working hours, then you should be able to anticipate them and set your mindset to dismiss them if necessary once they have shown themselves up.

Think of your past experience in working and ask the question to yourself: what are the things that usually distract me the most from my work? What are the things that I spend a lot of time doing in my working hours that are actually not related at all to the job that I do?

It should be noted though that sometimes the distractions can be necessary to be not avoided. Talking with co-workers, for example, can be an activity that build and improve the relationship that you have with them which in turn can benefit you and them in terms of teamwork for the jobs that you do together or conversation by using message apps are sure needed when there are any urgent things that you need to attend to. But if those activities besides your work are done for a significant portion of your working hours and they can make you run out of time for the work that you should do, then it is time to limit those activities that make you do not have enough time to produce a great work results. That is because it means you have already given in to the urge of procrastination too much and the consistency aspect of your work has already been significantly disturbed by the distractions.

When you define the things that can distract you from your work, you should:

- Note them in a list that you can view at any time. That way you do not forget what are the things that can take a significant amount of your working hours and you can anticipate them better during your work

- Make the list of the distractions a live list. When you find something which you have not noted but can actually distract significantly and give you urge to procrastinate for a long time, then you can add them to the list that you must try to avoid when you need to focus on your work

- Commit to stay away from the distractions in your list. It can be hard at first as you get used to do them in your working hours. However, if you want to optimize your work, get things done faster, and build a strong anti-procrastination mentality, then you should do what you can to at least avoid to do them in a long period during your working hours

- Put them away from your reach if the distractions are brought by tangible things. If you are often distracted by the things that are not used in your work but make you procrastinate, then you should keep them away from your sight and reach at least in the working hours. That way you will be less likely to be distracted by them

- Pay attention to only the things that distract you significantly. As being told before, some of the things that you think a distraction can be just for a short duration and can be put in a seldom frequency for you to do it so it should not count as the thing that you should avoid to do. Some of them even have a direct or indirect benefit to your work as that case of building a relationship with your co-worker before. Keep in mind about this and list only the things that you find tempting to do and waste a significant amount of your working hours. Do not use this point as an excuse for the things that are actually significant distractions but you still want to do in your working hours, though.

To give you some ideas about the things that you can list as distractions that you should keep away from doing for far too long, here are the things that are usually significant in distracting people from their work:

- Browse to some fun websites
- Scroll social media
- Talk with your peers about things unrelated to work
- Go out of the office for some purposes, e.g. going to the mini-markets, just walk around, etc
- Play games alone or with peers
- Use messaging apps

By limiting yourself to do the activities that significantly distract your attention from your work during the working hours, you can increase your productivity and build the consistency aspect in your anti-procrastination mentality in a major way.

Clear Your Thoughts

There is also another kind of distraction that can take away your working hours by preventing it to be productive besides external distractions like social media or games. It is the internal distraction that comes from within your thinking and distracts your mind to focus on the things that you work on.

This internal distraction can come in any form: the problems in other matters that are unrelated to your work (probably some personal or family problems), some things about the future that makes you worry about it, the news that you have just seen from television this morning, that social media post about something that you find really interesting, and many other things. These can clout your mind and makes you unable to concentrate fully on your work during the working hours. They can make you dumbfound yourself with the distracting thinking that come from those many sources.

An advice for you about that: don't do that! A cluttered mind can be an important factor that makes your work becomes inefficient and ineffective in terms of the time spent in it and can make you procrastinate significantly as you let your mind wander to the things that should be thought at other times or even should not be given attention at all.

What can you do, though, so you can clear your thoughts and focus fully to consistently put in high quality of effort in the work that you do? Here are some suggestions for you:

- Take a note about the things that distract your mind currently. It can be the things in the past that you worry about or the things in the future that you expect to happen. If it distracts your mind from the work that you do, then write it down somewhere to help you clear your mind from it

- Meditate daily. This activity is often attributed to the clear mind that someone can have as a result of doing it. Try to spare a little of your time in a day (outside of working hours, preferably) to meditate and see the result as you clear your mind from this activity

- Let go of the things that you should not think about. There can be some matters that distract your mind that should not be there in the first place. By choosing to let them go, you can be a step ahead to clear your mind from the things that you should not even bother

- Put aside some time to think and act on the matters that you concern about outside or inside your working hours. Things that are not related to work should be finished outside your working hours. If it is very urgent, then it is probably better you should excuse yourself or to the other people that you need to ask to for attending those problems you can be in peace with the matters. If it is something that is related to work, then you can finish them first in your working hours if it bothers your mind so much before you do other things

- Browse and watch less especially in the working hours. By limiting the access to the info that you actually do not need from the mass media, that should be able to help you limit your thinking to the things that matter the most to your work. It will be great if you can restrain yourself completely to not see them in the working hours too.

A clear mind should be able to focus more on the present and the things that you do in work. By having unclouded thinking, it should help you to optimize the time that you have for your work and avoid the procrastination that can be triggered by thinking about unimportant or unrelated things to work for too much.

Set Up the Barrier

This approach can be related to the optimization of the working environment where and when you do your job which has been described in deep in the "Optimize Work Context" chapter of the book. You should try to set your work context also so it can limit the distractions that you can get while you work.

Be it the place, the time, or the method that you can associate with the work that you do, they can also be optimized so they can prevent the distractions that you can have at work. By doing that optimally, you should be able to avoid the urge of procrastination even before they can come to you.

The way to do that can be unique according to your situation. If you are often distracted by your peers discussing about the things that are unrelated to work, for example, then you can move yourself to another place in your office where you can be alone and focus on doing your work if necessary. If you have a strong urge of procrastination in the form of browsing or social media when you are near the connection of the internet, then, if your work and other people around you do not need the connection, you can turn off the internet connection in your place for a while to accomplish your job in the day. That way, you can set up a powerful barrier to the distractions that often cause you to waste a lot of your working hours.

Time and method can also be factors in your barrier. If possible and you have flexible working hours, then you probably should place the period for you to work in a time when there are most minimum number of distractions for your job. You should also do the work method that causes you the minimum disturbance and can make you waste as little time as possible in your work. For example, if you find that meetings and do coordination with your peers via email can be highly ineffective and trigger unnecessary distractions for you such as a vast amount of unrelated discussion to the work, then probably you should think of other ways that can make your work significantly produce more results while not missing the advantages that you can get from the methods that you want to ditch.

One thing that should be noted, though, is that you should not be too extreme about it. When you work in an office, it is probably not a good idea to find a place to be alone all the time because you are distracted by the talking of your peers as you lose social relationship with them. The important thing is to be balanced and set the barrier when it is appropriate. Set your work context to be able to protect you from the urge of procrastination in a good way. The extreme should be reserved for a special time, probably when there is a very tight deadline in your work and you need to completely focus to be able to get things done better.

Set up a necessary and possible barrier to your work can be a way to significantly reduce the urge of procrastination given by the distractions that can be found around your work environment. Just remember to be sensible about it and work on the things that can significantly optimize your work.

****

Move away from distractions support your work consistency and limit your access to the significant procrastination urge. Define the distractions, clear your mind, and set up the necessary barrier to do that will improve the focus that you need to do your job also.

After this, we will move to the last part of the focus pillar in the bid to build a continuation aspect in a strong anti-procrastination mentality. It will focus on how you can shape a positive mindset to the things that prevent you from achieving success in your work.

FOCUS BUILD 3 – CONTINUATION: LOOK AT THE POSITIVE

When you meet some struggles or failures that hinder the progress in your work, especially the ones that have a significant impact to the things that you work on, you can feel that everything is negative and there is nothing that you can do to feel positive to the work that you do and the results that it produces. This, of course, can result in heavy procrastination as a result of the stress and frustration that is felt towards the work that you do.

In this particular kind of time, though, it becomes even more important for you to have a positive mindset and look at the positive side in your situation. The reason is mostly by doing that, you can have more chance to work again to do the things that need to be done for solving and overcoming the problems that you have. After all, only by putting in the necessary effort that you can change the bad situation that you are currently in into a good one.

Look at the positive side of the bad events that happen to you can also bring the confidence back to your ability so you are be able to get out of the current bad situation and give you the motivation that you need to work. Doing that can also push you to take the lessons that can be had from your struggles so you can improve yourself significantly and come back as a person who is more worthy of the success that you want in your work.

It can, understandably, sometimes hard to get out of the negativity that has affected our mind as a result of the problems that we face at our work and look at the positive side. You can say: What are the things that can be good if I get fired from the job that I had? What is the positive side that I can see if I fail massively in my business and go bankrupt? Events like this can be hard to navigate and it can be difficult for us to still have a positive mindset at times like these.

But, when you think deeper about it, then maybe you can find some positive things about your situation and even there is no to little content to it, this probably is an event that you need to experience in order to become successful in the future. Possibly you should pursue a different approach compared to the previous thing that you work on. Maybe when you are fired from your work, you can have severance package that you need to keep supporting your family while starting the business that you always want. Maybe when you have a bankruptcy as a result of your failed work in business, you can take valuable lessons from it so you can have a greater chance of success in the next venture of yours using the things that you have learned. Probably it sounds cliché but it can be the best thing that you can do to get out of the bad situation that you are in. The most important thing is, of course, to take as many lessons as possible from the setbacks that you have, try to always have a positive mindset, and keep the motivation to continue to work. Do not fall deep in procrastination because when you procrastinate in this kind of situation, it can be much harder for you to get back as it can be hard for you to trigger motivation to work again.

To help you keep the positive mindset even at the lowest setbacks that you can have in life so you can maintain the continuation aspect in your anti-procrastination mentality, there are some suggestions related to this that you can do: see the progress that you have made until you get to the point of setbacks and choose to keep going, learn what you can from the bad experience and move on, and push even harder with the effort to make it in your work. We will take discuss deeper each of the points next.

See the Progress and Keep Going

There must be some progress, either small or big, that you have made in your work related to the targets that you set. It is the progress which can get you this far to the point where the setback happens. That is a sign that you have done something related to your work and you must continue to work if you want to continue making progress.

Sometimes, it can be hard to see that you have done anything meaningful in your work if you experience failure. The things that you have put in the effort on seem do not result in anything and all of the tasks that you have accomplished seem to be in vain.

However, when you look back again from the starting point of your work and compare it with the point which you find yourself at during the bad situation that you are currently in, you will see that at least you have done something related to your work and have made some move forward. After all, it is impossible you fail if you have not done anything, however small, in your work.

It means that there is already a move forward in your journey towards the results that are desired as a result of the work that you do. Now, what should you do to keep on making the progress and advance forward? Of course, the answer is you need to get over your urge to procrastinate from the setbacks that you have and you need to keep on working hard so you can see more progress related to the targets that you want to achieve in your work.

Realize that there is something that can be felt as a result of your work can be good for your motivation. This should also make you be able to see the positive that you have made from your labor.

To be able to get more positive things from this practice of seeing the progress that you have made, here are some things that you can do:

- Remember the small or big successes that you have made. There can be some results that you have got from the work before you are in the setback point that can be associated with happy memories. Recall them during the setback to make you believe more in your ability to produce great things in the jobs that you do

- Reminisce all the works that you have done until now. Even if you probably have not achieved any successes that you can count, you can still reflect on all the works that you have done. By doing that, you can see that there is some progress that you made compared to your starting point

- Recall all the lessons learned that you have got so far in your work experience. Besides being able to remember your progress, some of them might be the solution to the bad situation that you find yourself in currently

- Think about the tough times that you have faced before in your work and how you have the motivation to come back from those. This might not be the first time that you have to face failures and struggles at work. You can draw inspiration from that on how you can get back up before after you hit the wall the previous time

- Evaluate how closer you are to your targets since you first start your work and it will be such a shame if you do not keep on going as soon as possible. Even in the midst of failure, you must have collected experience, knowledge, and skills in your work that will be very useful if you can keep maintaining your hard work to overcome the situation and continue. Quitting and falling deep to procrastination now means you will waste those things that you have got as an accumulation of the work that you have done before

You have done pretty well to get until this point so it will be a shame if you stop doing your work. You should be strong enough to move on from there and work hard again so you can overcome your problems to keep moving forward.

Learn and Move On

In the failures and struggles that you have, there must be some lessons that you can take as there is something you do which is not right that makes you in the situation such as now. That is okay and you should take the lessons that it gives to correct the approach to your work and move on.

As they say, you can learn more in your failures than in your success. By recognizing the mistakes that you have made, knowing what can you do to make it right, and resolving that you will not make the same mistakes again in the future because you do not want to experience the same bad situation again, you should have enough things from that evaluation process to bounce back and work better next time.

The most important thing after you learn from your mistake, however, is that you act on the lessons. If you procrastinate after the failures that you have faced and abandon your work, then the experience that you get from it will be for nothing and you cannot continue to progress yourself. It is very important to implement what you have learned and thought about the solution to the problems as quickly as you can. Delaying it can also mean that you could have already forgotten what you think you know based on the mistake that you do in the work.

Failures can happen a lot of times before you achieve the targets that you want in your work and each of these should develop yourself and the approach to the work that you do. You should be ready for all of the bad experiences, take the lessons, and move on. Make it your focus to the lessons that your failure in work can bring to be able to perfect yourself.

For the focus on the lessons learned from those struggles, here are some things that you can do to amplify the learnings for your work:

- Take note of the lessons that you have learned and keep it somewhere that you can look back to. The learnings can be something valuable that you need for your personal development at work. By writing them down, you should be able to recall them more clearly when you need it
- Trial and error on the solutions if needed and the condition allows. There can be some times when the solution that you think will work to overturn the failures might not work. If the condition allows, then you should try to do trial and error and see which of the solution that you can think of is the best for the situation. Do it fast so you can learn the lessons from this activity quickly
- Formalize your learnings in the form of something tangible in work. It can be something like an SOP if you fail because of the unorganized approach in the work of your business or new software that you must use the next time in work because the problem that causes the failure is because of a highly inefficient approach to the work that can actually be solved using technology. Either way, it is best to have something that you can show as learnings from your failure so you can be surer that it will not happen again in the future

- Reflect on the lessons learned too during your daily and periodic evaluation. If you run the progress tracking and reflection that has been suggested in the previous chapter, then you should also try to remember the learnings that you have got during the time when you meet problems in your work. That should emphasize them more in your mind while enhancing your learnings by thinking deeper on the problems and solutions during the reflection activity

- Implement what you have learned in discipline. There can be a point in the future when you have overcome the failures in work and are already in some period past it, then you forget the lessons and go back to your previous way of work before the struggles happen. Try to keep a reminder to yourself to stay disciplined in applying the lessons that you have learned and make it a habit for you to do it so you do not fall on the same mistakes twice in your work

Focus on learning and moving on from the mistakes that you have done in your work as fast as possible should be a powerful way to maintain continuation in your work for a strong anti-procrastination mentality that you shape.

Get on With the Effort

One of the positive things to focus on when you have a failure in work besides your progress and learnings is the effort that you need to put in as soon as possible to set things right and get yourself out of the trouble that you find yourself in.

After all, the crucial thing to remember is that you cannot get out of the failure without any effort in work. There is no one that can make you overcome the problems but yourself.

That is why it is so important too to keep yourself from procrastinating also when you do fail. By relaxing or doing other things in your working hours because you feel upset about the struggles that you face in work, you will only reduce the chance that you have to get back from the setbacks and keep on improving in your work.

When you try to put in the effort after you fail, though, remember that you probably have to change your approach in work so you can successfully navigate your way out of the trouble that you have had. Applying the lesson as you have learned in the previous part should be important in terms of modifying your approach. Thus, besides coming back from the trouble that you are in, you can be better against the same situation that causes you your current failure in the future.

It can be understandably hard, though, for you to focus on quickly getting back on work again after you have faced something which is a massive failure for you. Therefore, here are some suggestions that can make you focus on the effort that you have to put in your work again:

- Remember that the longer that you wait to act, the longer it will be that you are in the same situation. A bad situation cannot change on its own. By delaying your come back, you will delay your overturn from the bad situation that you face currently
- Review the possibility that it might take a little bit of a chance or effort for you to succeed. The amount of work that you have to put in is different depending on the failure that you face. Who knows that it only needs small things in your work in order to overturn the failure into success? You can never know that for sure until you try
- Think about the effect that it can give to you and other people if you keep dwelling on your failure

without any effort in your work to overturn it. The one who suffers because of that maybe not only you but also the people close to you. By getting to work quicker, you should be able to come back from the situation faster too

Have it in your mindset about the importance of working to overcome your setbacks can be the important factor that makes you can change the failure to the stepping stone that you need for your success. Your failure point might be closer to the success point in your work than you think. Therefore, keep the continuity of your work instead of procrastinating to find that out. Keep going forward so you can be able to get the results that you want in your work.

FINAL WORDS: WHEN WILL YOU START BUILDING THE MENTALITY?

For everything, there must be a start. The point where you begin from zero until you build your way step-by-step to eventually reach what you want to.

It can be very easy for us to fall to the trap of procrastination when we work. After all, the enjoyment that we feel is much better if we choose to procrastinate rather than if we work. It is often the case of which one of the choices is going to make us happier directly at the moment. And when it comes to that, most of the time there can only be one winner for us.

As time is a finite resource to any person, the way we spend it at the moment will eliminate the chance to spend it in other ways. The time that has gone cannot be taken back and how we spend it in the present can determine the future that we have.

This also relates to the achievement of success too that we want to have in our work.

I mean, have you ever seen a successful person who sleeps his/her way to the achievement that he/she has accomplished? Or, has there been a case where a person accomplishes all that he/she truly wants in life and one of the reasons for the accomplishment is no effort that is being put into it? No matter where you look, if there is something meaningful that is attained, then there must be a lot of work behind it. Possibly a long-time work that has taken the person years of labor until that person achieved the point of success that he/she did now.

Now, what happens if that successful person procrastinates a lot and does not consistently work hard to achieve the success that he/she wants or if there is no effort spared by the person who has achieved something big in life? For sure, there will be no success or achievement for him/her currently.

Procrastination can be the main thing that separates us from the success that we want. That is why it is so important for every person to avoid the urge of procrastination as much as possible when working. It is also part of the reasons why this book has been written and published so it can be read by you who are eager to build a strong anti-procrastination mentality in yourself. I hope by reading the book from the start until this point, you can have what you need to build a strong anti-procrastination mentality that can help you in optimizing your working hours to accomplish the labor that you want to do and achieve the success that you want to have by doing that.

Let's have a quick review on what we have learned so far in the book related to the anti-procrastination mentality, shall we?

At the beginning of the book, we have learned the detailed explanation of why giving in to procrastination can reduce the chance that we have for success significantly. We have discussed the very bad relationship between the two of them and how choosing to procrastinate can slow down your progress in work significantly, make you much closer to failure, and motivate you to quit completely from the work that you do. Those things are important matters that can explain why success can be much harder to get if we choose the way of procrastination in work.

After that, we learned about the 3Cs aspects that help to define the anti-procrastination mentality that we want. They are the Cause, Consistency, and Continuation. We have discussed how by having them in our work, we can have a much better prevention to the urge of delaying and abandoning work that can often come in our working hours.

Next, we discussed the three pillars that support the anti-procrastination mentality: Motivation, Build, and Focus. We understood deeper about the definition for each of them and why by applying them in our work, we can foster our growth in the 3Cs that define a strong anti-procrastination mentality earlier. We have looked at the detailed ways about how each of the pillars can contribute to each of the Cs by understanding how to make them stronger in relation to our work. This is important because the stronger each of the pillars that we have, the better it should be for the shaping of our anti-procrastination mentality. By understanding and doing the things that are suggested in these parts of the book for each pillar that supports the 3Cs, you should be able to give a much stronger preference to your work rather than comply with the urge of procrastination that you might have.

While I have tried to give the best suggestions that I can think of for you to build a powerful anti-procrastination mentality to optimize your time at work in this book, it is up to you to implement them and see the difference that they can make. The things that are given in the pages of this book will be just words and something that you remember vaguely in your mind if you do not try to practice what is suggested in it. The anti-procrastination mentality can only be built bit by bit with the discipline of doing the things that can prevent you from giving in to the urge of procrastination. That is something that should be done from time to time in your working hours. Only you who can decide that it is the right time to do that and become a person who is highly productive to reach the targets that you have set yourself in your work.

After all, I think we will all be better and benefit if every one of us has a strong barrier to procrastination in work and optimize the time that we have to do the things that can be done.

I mean imagine if every person in the world chooses to be productive and employ the anti-procrastination mentality for him/herself. What will be the effect of this change? I think the world can be a much better place as a result of the optimal work results from all of us and each of us can be much happier and fulfilled as a result of having a high possibility of achieving the success that he/she wants in life. That is a life which is much more satisfying for every one of us and that can happen because we have worked hard consistently in the job that we do every day. Every successful person should know that it should be just a matter of when, not if, we can achieve the success that we want from our work when we do our relentless and tireless pursuit for it.

That situation where every person has his/her life more fulfilled can start with you and your work. Build a strong anti-procrastination mentality of your own and see your work optimized as you progress closer and closer to the success that you want. That should be the way for you to get the most from the time that you have.

After all, we do not live in the cavemen era where we need procrastination to keep safe from danger, right? In fact, it might be that you can endanger yourself much more if you do not work and give in often to the urge of procrastination as you flirt with the failure in the work that you do.

Thus, start to shape your mentality now and be consistent with it. I hope that you eventually can build a strong anti-procrastination mentality for the work that you do!

DID YOU LIKE THE ANTI-PROCRASTINATION MENTALITY?

First of all, thanks to you, the reader of this book, who has taken the time to digest its content. I hope that anything that you have learned from this book will be useful for you and give you the support that you need to build a strong anti-procrastination mentality!

The feedback from you are very valuable to me as an author in the form of reactions, comments, suggestions, or others. This is for the knowledge of mine whether the book hits the spot for you or not or there is something that I have to take note of for my future books. If you have something that you want to say about this book or if you happen to love the book content, then consider to tell them by giving your reviews at the Amazon page of this book. I promise you that I will read all of them!

MORE BOOKS BY DAN KRISTOPH

*****

How to Do What You Love: 3 Phases for Working with Passion and Achieve Success

Overcoming Failure: How to Turn Failure into Success

Do More Better Faster: The Optimal Outcomes Approach on How to be More Productive and Get More Done in Less Time

Stop Overthinking: How to Relieve Anxiety Stop Worrying and Reduce Stress

The To-Do List Formula: The Guide to Create a To-Do List that Improves Productivity and Makes You Achieve Success

*****

You can see more about the books by visiting his Author Central Page in Amazon:
http://amazon.com/author/dankristoph

ABOUT THE AUTHOR

The right self-improvement can give you a strong base to achieve what you want in life.

Do you want to be a better person and have a better life? The power of positive habits can help you significantly for that. The condition of your life seems to be created by the habits that you try to implement consistently. The positive habits can propel you to the life that you desire while the bad ones can make you stuck in a bad condition.

Having taking a liking on the subject of self-improvement, drawing the inspiration from the many books that he has read on the topic and the lessons that he has learned through his own life experience, Dan Kristoph tries to share the unique perspective that he has on self-improvement areas in each of his books. Every book that he has written contains comprehensive description and practical suggestions on what are the positive habits that can help you in many aspects of life. Hopefully by reading some of his books, you can learn and practice the habits that you need to make a better and more positive version of life that you want for yourself.

When he is not writing a book, Dan loves to read self-improvement books (obviously), watch movies, and travel. He loves to joke also though sometimes he is the only one who laughs on it :(

You can visit his blog, Positivity Stories, by visiting the below link:
http://positivitystories.com